2009

The Open University

Block 5

Making care safer?

K101 An introduction to health and social care

2009

This publication forms part of an Open University course K101 *An introduction to health and social care*. Details of this and other Open University courses can be obtained from the Student Registration and Enquiry Service, The Open University, PO Box 197, Milton Keynes MK7 6BJ, United Kingdom: tel. +44 (0)845 300 60 90, email general-enquiries@open.ac.uk

Alternatively, you may visit the Open University website at www.open.ac.uk where you can learn more about the wide range of courses and packs offered at all levels by The Open University.

To purchase a selection of Open University course materials, visit www.ouw.co.uk or contact Open University Worldwide, Walton Hall, Milton Keynes MK7 6AA, United Kingdom for a brochure: tel. +44 (0)1908 858793; fax +44 (0)1908 858787; email ouw-customer-servicesopen.ac.uk

The Open University
Walton Hall
Milton Keynes
MK7 6AA

First published 2008.

Edited and designed by The Open University.

Typeset in India by Alden Prepress Services, Chennai.

Printed and bound in Malta by Gutenberg Press Limited.

ISBN 978 0 7492 4646 4

1.1

Contents

Learning skills by Andrew Northedge

Introduction to Block 5

In this block you will be focusing on some of the ways in which care can be made safer, for both service users and health and social care workers. There will always be risks in health and social care settings, and unexpected events that are beyond anyone's control. It is impossible to make care absolutely safe but you can try to make care as safe as possible.

'Making care safer' doesn't mean just keeping people physically safe, although that is obviously very important. Of course, measures must be taken to prevent nurses from developing back problems through lifting patients, and to ensure that people with dementia don't get run over by passing traffic. But making care safer is also about making sure that care workers:

- are properly recruited and trained
- have the right information about service users
- offer care that is likely to work and not harm service users
- know their roles and responsibilities
- know what procedures to follow for common situations
- know who to turn to if they are in difficulties
- are properly monitored and supervised
- understand issues to do with confidentiality and information sharing
- are accountable for their actions.

It is also about making sure that service users:

- have access to good-quality information to help them make choices about their care
- know what has happened in the past and why
- know what to expect in the future.

The question mark in the title of this block, 'Making care safer?', is there because I hope that the block will help you think about whether some of the ways in which people try to make care safer actually have that effect.

The first unit in the block (Unit 17) is called 'Unacceptable care'. It explores some common dilemmas and difficulties in care settings and considers how they can lead to poor-quality and unsafe care being provided. The unit focuses particularly on intimate care.

Unit 18 'Handling personal information' examines personal information about service users. You will think about the role that record keeping plays in making care safer and the ways in which computers are changing the nature of personal records. You will also begin to look at sharing information about service users and handling confidential information.

In Unit 19 'Getting care right' you will examine how service users and care workers can work out the best thing to do in a particular situation to ensure that the care provided will benefit service users and not harm them.

Unit 20 is the skills unit for the block. You will develop your understanding of working with personal information by doing a series of activities based on a confidentiality policy, as well as practising some study skills.

Unit 17

Unacceptable care

Prepared for the course team by Rebecca Jones,
Hilary Brown and Andrew Northedge

Contents

Introduction

Block 5 focuses on making care safer. This unit begins to address this theme by looking at some of the common ways in which care can be unsatisfactory, of poor quality, or unsafe. Later units in the block focus on some of the ways in which care can be made safe and of high quality, but here you are going to examine how and why care that is unacceptably poor can come about.

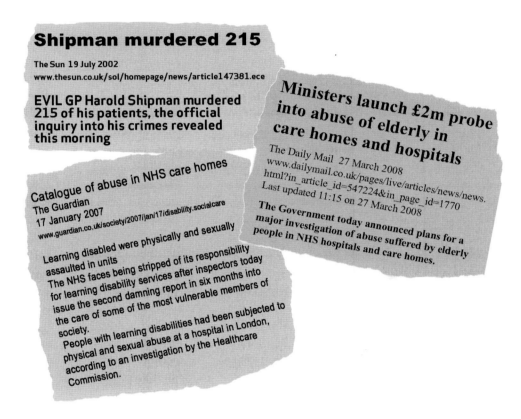

Shipman murdered 215

The Sun 19 July 2002
www.thesun.co.uk/sol/homepage/news/article147381.ece

EVIL GP Harold Shipman murdered 215 of his patients, the official inquiry into his crimes revealed this morning

Ministers launch £2m probe into abuse of elderly in care homes and hospitals

The Daily Mail 27 March 2008
www.dailymail.co.uk/pages/live/articles/news/news.
html?in_article_id=547224&in_page_id=1770
Last updated 11:15 on 27 March 2008

The Government today announced plans for a major investigation of abuse suffered by elderly people in NHS hospitals and care homes.

Catalogue of abuse in NHS care homes

The Guardian
17 January 2007
www.guardian.co.uk/society/2007/jan/17/disability.socialcare

Learning disabled were physically and sexually assaulted in units
The NHS faces being stripped of its responsibility for learning disability services after inspectors today issue the second damning report in six months into the care of some of the most vulnerable members of society.
People with learning disabilities had been subjected to physical and sexual abuse at a hospital in London, according to an investigation by the Healthcare Commission.

Scandals about poor-quality, unsafe and even abusive care are regularly reported in the media. Sometimes these terrible situations seem to have arisen mainly because a particular individual was ill intentioned, as appears to have been the case with Harold Shipman, a GP who is thought to have murdered at least 215 of his patients. But, more commonly, poor-quality, unsafe or abusive care occurs not because individual care workers are ill intentioned but through a combination of everyday problems. For example:

- Care workers may be busy, distracted, not confident in their role, unclear about their responsibilities or undertrained.

- Care workers may find particular service users unsympathetic or difficult to work with.

- Carers may have difficulties in their relationship with the person they are caring for.

- Workplaces may build up a negative culture in which bad practice becomes normal.

Often, poor practice occurs in care situations that are challenging to the care worker, for example giving intimate care or dealing with challenging behaviour. Most people who work in care settings do their best, but will sometimes have reached the end of their tether with a particular service user, perhaps after a particularly difficult shift. If you have done formal or informal care work, you may be able to remember times when the care you provided was not really good enough. Most carers don't let difficulties tip over into violent actions or open aggression towards the people they are caring for, but they may well have felt near to it, or have felt like switching off or walking away. Understanding the factors which come together to create these 'near misses' is an important step towards minimising risk and preventing flashpoints from occurring in your family, professional relationships or service settings.

This unit can provide only an introduction to a very complicated subject but it will help you to begin thinking about how and why care goes wrong. It will help you to consider situations in more depth, not merely blaming 'them' but seeing how all of 'us' carry within us both the potential for harming others and also the resources to step back and resolve difficulties in a more constructive way.

I have called this unit 'Unacceptable care' because it covers a wide range of situations, from those which could be described as 'perfectly ordinary but unsatisfactory' to those which are definitely abusive. What is acceptable may vary between individuals and situations, as you will see, so an important question is always 'unacceptable to whom and in what circumstances?'

In the first section you will look at what it is like for service users to receive intimate care that is not acceptable to them. In the second section you will consider some of the dilemmas and difficulties that can arise for care workers when offering intimate care, and how this affects the safety and quality of care. The third section turns to situations in which care can easily become abusive or unsafe – when service users are violent, unpredictable or abusive. The final section looks at how workplaces can develop cultures that are abusive and how individual care workers can get sucked into those cultures. It also introduces ways in which care workers can respond to those situations.

Core questions

- How can intimate care be provided in ways that make people feel comfortable and safe?

- Why can offering intimate care be embarrassing and difficult?

- What are the implications of describing someone's behaviour as 'challenging'?

- How can workplace cultures contribute to poor-quality and abusive care?

Are you taking the IVR?

If you are studying K101 as part of the Integrated Vocational Route (IVR), don't forget to check your VQ Candidate Handbook to see which Unit 17 activities contribute to your electronic portfolio.

1 Receiving intimate care

You begin your exploration of care that is not good enough by thinking about the experience of receiving intimate care.

1.1 Being on the receiving end

Read the following case study, which comes from an interview with someone who found herself temporarily needing intimate care.

Elspeth Grant

I had an accident and I fell which resulted in both my wrists being broken and my chest bone and my sternum. So, in seconds I went from fully fit, completely looking after myself to being dependent. So it was really, really quite a shock.

I was on holiday but I came home three days later. The plane journey was absolutely horrific. That was my first experience of having to look after myself where nobody could help. My sister, who was with me, could take me to the toilet but she couldn't on the plane because the toilets on planes are so small. It was a long plane journey and when I got home my 21-year-old daughter opened the door and I saw the fear in her eyes. Really the fear in her eyes, 'cos here was her mother standing here with two big plasters on. I looked dreadful because I hadn't slept but also I was wet, you know, I'd been, not incontinent but I could not dry myself after going to the toilet. My clothes were wet and that feeling, I think, was one of the worst feelings I have ever had in my life. I couldn't do anything about it. I was smelling.

[After several days' delay, Elspeth eventually started receiving some formal care services.]

This wee girl arrived and she was from the private agency because social work were too busy. This wee girl, as very kind as she was, she didn't seem to have any training and she had no gloves, she had no apron, absolutely nothing, no protection with her. And I got into the shower and I had to direct her, and of course she couldn't really wash me if she had no gloves and that was what I was needing. It was really hard having to stand naked in the shower in front of a stranger. I thought 'my goodness me' but I just had to do it. I had to do it but none the less the embarrassment of all of that, never mind that I couldn't get washed properly either.

When the social care assistant came, the difference was phenomenal. This woman, Fiona, was tremendous, she'd done the job for 17 years or something and she knew what she was about. She obviously knew what she was doing, she came with very good eye contact, very businesslike approach but friendly. Knew my name, knew what she was there for, had known that I had had an accident. You know, she knew about me before she came. The girls from the agency were just sent to help me. Fiona knew about me so communication was better there, and that was what made the difference. She was well resourced, she had an apron and gloves, etc. And, you know, when it came to washing you intimately that wasn't a problem, it was just dealt with. She always made sure I was well covered with my dressing gown over my shoulders to walk back into the bedroom to get dressed. But the others, you know, wouldn't have thought of that.

Fiona's counterpart – there was two of them because they worked four days on and four days off – she was a very nice lady too and I have no doubt would have been as well trained but on the three occasions that she came to my door she was always late, she was always busy, she came in the door 'Oh, really busy today' and on the three occasions I just said to her 'It's OK, I can manage today'. Because I didn't want that hassle, she was so busy. Perhaps that wasn't the impression she meant to give, but that was the way I was, you don't want to be a bother. I mean Fiona would have been just as busy because she had the same case load but her whole demeanour was that she was there for me, this is a time for me.

(Personal communication)

Some of the care Elspeth received was of good quality and acceptable to her. She clearly liked and trusted Fiona and felt that she was getting the support she needed from her. But the rest of her care was much less good.

Activity 1   Why was this unacceptable?
Allow about 15 minutes

Make some notes to answer these two questions:

(a) In what ways was the care Elspeth received poor quality? (You might find it helpful to think about what she says was good about Fiona and what this implies about the other care workers.)

(b) What other factors made the whole experience difficult for Elspeth?

Comment

(a) Poor-quality care

- The care didn't start when Elspeth needed it, but only several days later.
- The person from the agency didn't seem to have received any training and didn't seem to know what she was doing.
- She had no protective equipment. This meant she couldn't actually help Elspeth wash properly, which was the main thing she wanted.
- She didn't help Elspeth deal with the embarrassment of being naked in front of a stranger. She didn't think of ways of decreasing the amount of time Elspeth spent naked.
- She didn't know anything about Elspeth before she met her – she seemed to be there just to 'help', without any clear idea of what that might entail.
- She didn't make good eye contact.
- Fiona's colleague was always late and gave the impression of being so busy that Elspeth preferred not to receive help from her at all.
- She didn't make Elspeth feel that this was her time to which she was entitled.

(b) Experience as a whole

- Elspeth made a sudden transition from being fit and well to being in considerable pain and without the use of both her hands.

- The toilet on the aeroplane was not accessible to someone needing assistance.

- By the end of the flight, Elspeth could smell stale urine on herself, and her clothes were wet with urine. She describes it as one of the worst feelings she has ever had in her life.

- Her daughter was clearly shocked by her appearance at the end of the flight.

Elspeth did not receive the care she needed from the agency worker or from Fiona's colleague. The care she did receive from them was not provided in a way that maintained her dignity. Nobody except Fiona seemed to be thinking about what it was like for Elspeth to receive care. She had gone suddenly from independence to needing intimate care and found the change understandably traumatic. Fiona had taken the time to find out about Elspeth before she visited and the effect of all her behaviour was to make Elspeth feel safe and appropriately cared for.

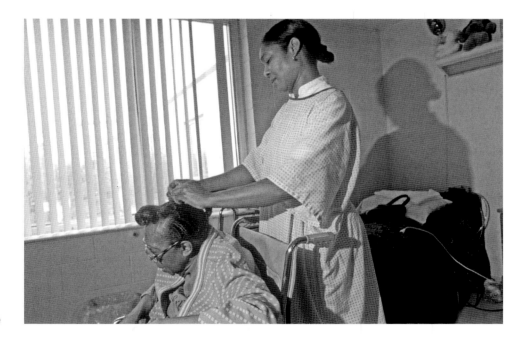

Intimate care – hair care

In the next activity you are going to think about how you would like your own intimate care to be handled.

Activity 2   What if it were you?

Allow about 10 minutes

Have you ever needed any intimate care? If so, think about what you liked and didn't like in your carer's approach. If you have never been on the receiving end of intimate care, think about how you would react to different ways of doing things.

- Would it help you if you had a sense that the carer was following a set procedure, or would you prefer them to ask how you wanted something done or how you would have done it yourself?

- Would you like your carer to keep their distance or would you prefer more of the human touch?

- What kind of words would you feel most comfortable using in such a situation? For example, children have their own vocabulary of 'wees' and 'poos' while other people may use medical terminology.

Comment

People who read the course had quite strong views on this. One person, who has had extensive experience of care at home, said it very much depended on the relationship with her carer. If the carer was someone she knew well, she would expect some humour. If she did not know the carer, she would feel much more comfortable with a formal approach. Another person said that she liked a fairly formal relationship with her carers even though she had known some of them for years, because it helped her feel less embarrassed at being naked or on the toilet. She preferred them to use medical terminology for body parts and functions. She didn't mind fitting into their procedures because she couldn't be bothered to keep explaining what she wanted. A third person said that he did want to be asked about how he wanted to be touched and handled; otherwise he felt like an item on a conveyor belt, not an individual. Another said that it was really important to her that her care provider was female.

Clearly, people vary in how they like to be treated when receiving intimate care. Providing good-quality care which helps someone maintain their dignity involves taking account of this. It would be unacceptable to use informal language and a jokey manner with the person who liked a formal relationship. The person who said he wanted to be asked about his preferences would not be receiving good-quality care if his carers just got on with their usual system. So taking account of service users' personalities, histories and preferences is an important way of making sure that they receive good-quality care.

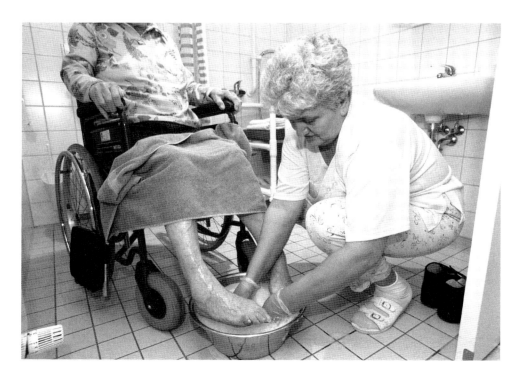

Intimate care – foot care

1.2 Negotiating boundaries

One of the things Elspeth found difficult was having to stand naked in front of a stranger. That's not something that happens often in ordinary life. Even intimate medical examinations usually involve only partial nudity and the careful deployment of screens and sheets. One of the things that makes intimate care so difficult is that it crosses the boundaries of normal social interaction (Twigg, 2006). Once these boundaries have been breached it can be difficult to work out where the new lines should be drawn.

Service users such as Elspeth can feel uncomfortable and embarrassed when these boundaries are breached, but so can care workers, as you will see in the next section. In a research study with disabled people (Meyer et al., 2007) it emerged that people who employ personal assistants have to learn how to manage their carers' uncertainty. Janet said:

> I guess part of my role is to be comfortable to say, 'Just go round there a bit more, rinse the washcloth off because it smells from there, and remember to go front to back …

(Meyer et al., 2007, p. 600)

Janet makes it sound easy, but even articulate disabled people who employ their own personal assistants find that boundaries can become blurred. One service user commented that even where she wanted to maintain a businesslike relationship:

> People cross over that business line within a few weeks. And then they feel like they're your best friend because they've helped you get your pants on in the morning.
>
> […]
>
> You have somebody doing intimate work for you … so they give you a little massage – is that OK or not OK? … they're always undressing you. That's how … things get gray. Things get strange.

(Quoted in Saxton et al., 2001, p. 401)

As this quote suggests, the line between what is care and what is sexual contact can become unclear when intimate care is being provided. Providing intimate care often involves direct physical touch and nakedness and sometimes gives rise to emotional closeness. These are also characteristics of sexual relationships, so it is not surprising that the boundaries between care and sex become blurred (Twigg, 2000, 2006). This can make it difficult for service users and care workers to work out what is acceptable behaviour and what is not.

You will look at this issue of boundaries and why intimate care is so challenging in more detail in the next section.

Key points

- Receiving intimate care can be embarrassing and uncomfortable for service users.

- It is important that individual service users are asked about their preferences and needs when receiving intimate care.

- Intimate care crosses over the boundaries of normal social interaction. This can make it difficult to work out what is acceptable behaviour and what is unacceptable.

2 Offering intimate care

In this section you will continue looking at the experience of intimate care but this time from the perspective of someone offering care.

Intimate care – help with washing

2.1 Personal and intimate care

In order to explore these issues, you are going to follow a young care worker, Marie O'Brien, during her first few months as a support worker at Millstream Court, a supported-living facility for young disabled people. Marie's story is based on real people in real situations, observed in research studies by one of the unit authors. Minor details have been changed so that the service cannot be recognised and the privacy of the service users is respected.

Getting into care work

Marie works in Millstream Court, a supported-living service for people with physical and learning disabilities run by a voluntary organisation. She previously trained in childcare at her local further education college. She did one of her placements at a day nursery which included children with learning disabilities and really enjoyed it. She was thrilled to get the job. It doesn't pay well but it is local and she can easily get there on the bus even for the early morning shift. Marie lives at home with her parents; she has been going out with her boyfriend, Jason, for two years and is saving up to get engaged.

At the interview the head of care asked Marie about person-centred plans and she was able to talk about the system used at the nursery for recording what each child liked and needed during the day. Marie's maturity and enthusiasm, along with good references, secured her the job.

Before her first shift, she went to meet some of the other workers, especially Joan, the senior care officer who would be her team leader. Joan introduced her to Richard and Fakhra as Marie was to be their key worker.

For the first week Marie was on day duty, which involved going to the young person's flat and getting them up, then helping them eat breakfast. On her first day she worked with Joan to help Fakhra get dressed. Fakhra needed a lot of help and, when breakfast arrived, Marie realised that she did not know how to help Fakhra eat. She looked round for assistance but Joan had already left to help someone else, so she 'owned up' to Fakhra, who grinned. When Marie put the food in too quickly Fakhra spat it out, but gradually Marie found the right speed and relaxed, and they seemed to be getting on well. Nevertheless, Marie wondered if there were specific skills she needed because sometimes the food went down the wrong way and twice Fakhra choked. Marie was afraid that she might accidentally hurt Fakhra despite doing her best.

Activity 3 What were the risks?

Allow about 10 minutes

What were the risks in someone as inexperienced as Marie being left to feed Fakhra? Jot down some notes about the risks to both Fakhra and Marie.

Comment

Most seriously, Fakhra choked twice. Choking can be very unpleasant and can occasionally lead to death. Marie might not have known what to do if someone is choking badly, or she might have known in principle from a first-aid course but never have had to intervene in reality. This would increase the risk that serious harm could come from Fakhra choking.

As it happened, Fakhra seemed to respond well to Marie's confession of ignorance, but there was a risk that she might have felt anxious or worried by Marie's ignorance. She might have lost her confidence in the quality of the care being offered by Millstream Court. She might have felt that her dignity was not being respected – choking is not dignified.

There were also risks to Marie. It didn't help her confidence in her ability to do her new job. If the worst had happened and Fakhra had choked to death, Marie would have been very traumatised. She would also have been involved in a disciplinary hearing and probably a court case or inquest, which would be very distressing.

Marie survived her first day. Although things did not go perfectly, having to ask Fakhra for help put their relationship on a good footing, making it more of a two-way process. But more challenging experiences were to come.

Marie's second day

On her second day, Marie was to get Richard up first. Richard had his own room and Marie knocked and went in. Joan had said Richard needed 'total care' but Marie wasn't quite sure what that meant. She knew he liked to work and play on his computer using a probe he wore around his forehead. She had been told that he could move from the bed to his wheelchair but would otherwise need help with dressing and toileting.

When Marie went to help Richard get up it was obvious that he had an erection. She didn't know what to do. She wondered if she should go out of the room or go to find Joan, but probably Joan would be busy and also Marie didn't know what she would say, so she decided to stay and just turn away for a bit. Eventually, she took Richard to the bathroom. By this stage she was confused as well as embarrassed. She realised that Richard was going to need help to go to the loo and saw the urinal bottles on the shelf. Since he could not use his hands she had to put his penis into the bottle and keep it there while he urinated. Then she took him back to his room and helped him to wash his face and get dressed.

She did not know how she should do all this – what tone of voice to use, whether to make a joke of it or take it seriously, whether to say anything or keep quiet, whether to lock the door or to leave it slightly ajar. She felt upset that she had not realised this would be involved in the job and when she got home she thought it best not to say anything in case Jason or her parents misunderstood. She thought Jason might tell her she should leave the job, so she kept her worries to herself. All the other staff just seemed to get on with the job and she didn't want to make a fuss. When her friends asked her about her new job she glossed over this aspect of it and talked about feeding Fakhra and going out shopping with other service users.

If Marie had a different sort of job – say in a bank or a shop – she would not be expected to take a man to the toilet or to see him naked. At Millstream Court everyone acted as if it was the most 'normal' thing in the world, but it wasn't normal in Marie's world.

Marie experienced one of the ways in which the boundaries between intimate care and sexual contact can become blurred and she had no preparation to help her know what to do or how to act. We don't know from this case study what Richard's feelings were, but he may have been embarrassed and uncomfortable too. Elspeth, in Section 1, found receiving intimate care from someone who was inexperienced and untrained much more embarrassing than care from Fiona. Richard may also have found that Marie's inexperience made the situation worse. Marie had encountered some of the hidden aspects of care work – the bits that are not easy to talk about – and the only way she could find to manage it was by turning away and keeping it to herself.

Later, over an end-of-shift cup of tea in the staff room, one of the other support workers who had previously worked with Richard said to Marie: 'Enjoy your first day with Richard then? He's well hung, isn't he?' The other workers, all women, laughed. Marie didn't know how to react. She felt a little uncomfortable, but decided the best thing she could do was to join in the giggles.

2.2 The demands of intimate care

What can you learn from Marie's first days at work? Why is this aspect of the work so challenging for her, and why does she seem so ill prepared for something that is so central to her new job? One way of thinking about it is that this part of the work jolts her out of her usual ways of relating. It requires more than just being 'nice', because it necessitates *breaking* the usual rules about how to behave in order to attend to bodily functions which we normally take a lot of trouble to keep private. In the study that you are about to read, by Jocelyn Lawler, it emerged that student nurses struggle, just as Marie did, with their first encounters with patients.

Reader

Activity 4   Understanding Marie's reaction to Richard

Allow about 25 minutes

Turn to Chapter 17, 'Body care and learning to do for others', by Jocelyn Lawler in the Reader (pages 137–45) and read pages 137–41 as far as the heading 'Learning "basic" nursing'. In this chapter Lawler describes the results of her research with nurses who are learning to manage intimate bodily care. Make notes to help you explain Marie's reactions to caring for Richard.

Here are some pointers to help you:

- The chapter starts by considering cultural issues. Make some notes about factors which make it difficult for some nurses to learn how to handle other people's bodies.

- Lawler discusses the significance of the naked male body to female nurses. Describe in your own words what she is saying.

- The nurses Lawler interviewed had had some training in carrying out a bed bath. Why was that not enough to enable them to manage intimate care with confidence?

Comment

Lawler observes that Western cultures, particularly British culture, are 'non-touching'. If nurses came from backgrounds that were more relaxed about touching, she argues, they had less difficulty in learning how to manage intimate care.

Lawler indicates that female nurses had more difficulty managing intimate care with men than with women, and indeed more difficulty than male nurses had with female patients. She argues that men's genitals are particularly problematic. They are normally hidden, except in sexual situations, so handling them breaks some deeply held social taboos.

The trainee nurses had had some training in the technical elements of carrying out a bed bath. But what they had to learn from experience was how to manage the 'social awkwardness' – no one taught them that.

In the light of this, Marie's reaction to the situation with Richard is easy to explain. Her situation was in many respects worse than that of the nurses Lawler interviewed. They at least had had training in how to do the work even if it did not include managing the awkwardness. Marie did not even have that.

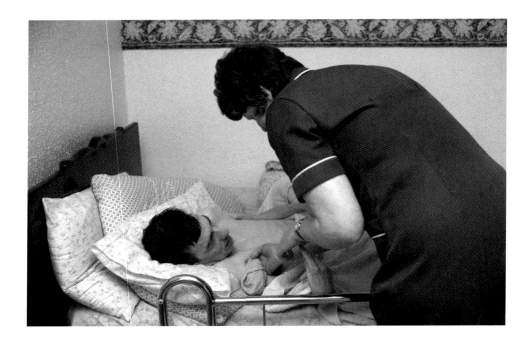

Intimate care – in bed

Compared with many care workers, Marie was fairly well trained in some aspects of her job. She had done a college course and had worked with disabled children in the past. However, nothing had prepared her for intimate care. As Lawler says of the trainee nurses:

> … they lacked skill and they encountered scenes for which they were completely unprepared. As a consequence they felt inadequate.

> (Reader, Chapter 17, p. 140)

Although intimate care is one of the most challenging areas of care work, it is hard to discuss. Marie feels that she cannot discuss it with colleagues, family or friends. Little effort seems to go into preparing workers or passing on tips for how they can manage their reactions appropriately. Typically, intimate care is provided by the most junior staff – as care workers are promoted and take on more responsibility, they do less and less direct work with service users' bodies (Twigg, 2006). Intimate care had not been mentioned in Marie's interview and her manager had not gone into detail about how this part of the work should be performed.

In the next activity you consider how this might be improved.

Reader

Activity 5   Learning how to do intimate care

Allow about 40 minutes

Read the rest of Chapter 17 in the Reader (pages 141–5) and then write down some suggestions about how to help Marie learn to manage situations like this, drawing on both the Reader chapter and your own thoughts.

Comment

I came up with the following ideas. It will help Marie if:

- She is taught the technical skills of, for instance, helping a man to urinate into a bottle.
- She has a longer period accompanying another worker, to watch how they manage Richard's intimate care and deal with aspects such as

maintaining as much privacy as possible. It will also help Marie if she has opportunities to discuss what she has been shown afterwards.

- She is encouraged to consider in advance how she might respond to a situation where she has to handle a man's penis, including one where he has an erection. She might be taught how to manage her own emotions. She might also be taught how to say to Richard that she will leave the room until his erection has gone.

- She is encouraged to think about the language to use when referring to body parts and functions; knowing what language or gestures Richard understands would be a good start.

Lawler's research shows that managing intimate care is a taboo subject not only in the residential care home where Marie works, but generally among people who do care work. Marie's role is poorly defined. Not many people would know exactly what a 'support worker' does. When she is not providing physical care she is supposed to act as a friend or equal to Fakhra and Richard, which means switching in and out of roles as she performs different aspects of her work.

From Marie's story you can see how learning how to manage intimate care may be poorly dealt with during induction into care work. She was expected just to get on with it. The only time it was discussed was as a joke at Richard's expense. Yet these tasks are a key part of the work. If they are performed by someone who is not well intentioned, or who has no experience or training, or who feels awkward or disgusted, they become occasions for potential abuse. Marie knows she has strayed into territory which her family and boyfriend would feel uncomfortable about and which she feels embarrassed to mention. Later this could also lead her to act insensitively, or alternatively to become so blasé that she forgets Richard's feelings. Writing about nursing, Lawler comments that:

> Nursing involves not only doing things which are traditionally assigned to females, and learning to do them by experience and practice, but also crossing social boundaries, breaking taboos and doing things for people which they would normally do for themselves in private if they were able.

(Lawler, 1991, p. 30)

This is an important area in the safety of care. Marie was well intentioned but she was also naïve and ill prepared. Had she been ill intentioned, she had every opportunity to exploit the situation with Richard – and who would know? Richard has very limited ability to communicate, and people might not have believed him if he had complained.

However, steps *are* being taken to address these skills more formally. For example, Skills for Care, the strategic development body for the adult social care workforce in England, has developed common induction standards, which all new social care workers and those changing jobs have to meet within twelve weeks of starting their new jobs (Skills for Care, 2005).

National Vocational Qualifications (NVQs) and Scottish Vocational Qualifications (SVQs) cover some aspects of intimate care. At least 50% of staff employed in care homes for adults must hold a VQ Level 2 (Department of Health (DH) 2003a, 2003b). Level 2 qualifications require care workers to demonstrate such skills as supporting someone to go the toilet, enabling them to maintain their personal hygiene, and supporting them in personal dressing and grooming. Level 3 qualifications cover skills such as helping people to move using specialist equipment, for example hoists, and changing catheter bags.

Kevin Madden and Elvis Malcolm from Somebody Cares help Brian Hole to wash

Personal assistants and training

Most people who receive care probably do want their care workers to be trained and experienced in their roles. However, some people who employ personal assistants (PAs) through Direct Payments and similar schemes explicitly want people who have not been trained in this sort of work. This is because they feel that people who have not been trained will be more responsive to their employers' wishes and will learn to do things in the way the service user wants, rather than imposing their own ideas.

For example, Louise Smith, a Direct Payments user says:

> The personal assistants who have never done 'care' work are always the best. They are respectful, responsive and have a whole different attitude about their work, and I get better quality assistance.

> (Leece and Bornat, 2006, p. 126)

Another study found that most Direct Payments users preferred to train their PAs themselves and resented it if PAs became too 'professional' in the way they behaved. One said:

> I don't like the idea of these people who've been told the right way to [do things] … I want to be treated as a human being and as an employer, not as a person to be cared for or done to.

> (Glendinning et al., 2000, p. 16)

However, this can cause difficulties if a PA wants formal training, either because they feel they cannot perform their current job properly without such training or because they want to improve their career prospects (Scourfield, 2005). It is important to balance service users' rights to receive care in the way they want with PAs' needs for training and career development.

Not all organisations provide as poor an induction as Millstream Court did for Marie. At Somebody Cares, the care agency based in Cardiff that you met in Block 1, a careful programme of induction for new staff is provided. This includes shadowing an experienced member of staff for a week during which they are shown how to undertake intimate care tasks. So, for example, when a care worker is giving someone a bed bath, the new member of staff will be shown how to cover the parts of the person's body which are not being washed with towels, so that they are not left naked. When taking someone to the toilet, they will be taught to shut the door and leave the person alone until they are called for.

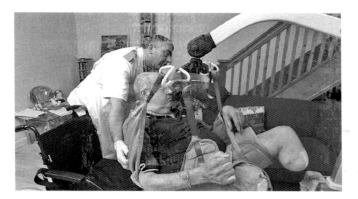

Kevin Madden from Somebody Cares helps Brian Hole to move safely by using a hoist

They are also shown how to use any hoists or equipment and told how important it is to wear gloves and aprons and use antibacterial handwashes.

This sort of practical demonstration of how to provide intimate care safely and with regard to someone's privacy and dignity would have greatly improved the care which Marie could offer and which Elspeth received.

Key points

- Care work can involve performing intimate tasks, such as toileting and dressing people.

- This aspect of the work is frequently hidden from view, and workers are ill prepared for it.

- Although care establishments are largely organised around the need to provide intimate care, this may not be acknowledged in the public face of the service, or reflected in its training, guidance or supervisory practice.

- When it comes to keeping care safe, it is important that intimate care work is appropriately supervised.

3 Challenging behaviour

In this section you will continue to think about the ways in which ordinary care situations involving well-intentioned care workers can tip over into unacceptable, unsafe and even abusive behaviour. You are going to look at situations in which a service user is behaving in ways that a care worker finds difficult to deal with; this in turn makes it difficult for the care worker to act in the best way.

Sometimes service users can behave aggressively or even violently

To begin with, spend a few minutes reflecting on your own experience in the following activity.

Activity 6   Not my finest hour

Allow about 15 minutes

Have you ever had to deal with someone who was being difficult or behaving badly, unreasonably or violently, and you didn't handle it very well? Perhaps you lost your temper in response. Here are some common situations that you might have experienced:

- a toddler having a tantrum
- a teenager behaving unreasonably or doing something forbidden
- someone you are caring for becoming violent or shouting at you
- a friend, family member or colleague blaming you for something you didn't think was your fault.

Or you might remember a different sort of occasion. It doesn't matter what you think of as long as it was a difficult situation where you feel you could have responded more constructively than you did. Make some notes about what the situation was and then answer the following questions.

- What did you do in response?
- How did it make you feel?
- What happened then?
- Can you see any ways things could have got even worse?

Comment

One course tester thought of a mealtime with her toddler son after a difficult day. He wouldn't sit down in his highchair, wouldn't wear a bib and then threw food all over the newly washed floor. She shouted and swore at him and tried to force the bib onto him. She remembers feeling very angry and thinking that he was doing it on purpose to wind her up. Her son began to cry and she burst into tears herself. She said that she could imagine several ways in which it might have got worse – she might have continued to try and force the bib on and have hurt her son in the process; she might have handled him so roughly that he banged against the table or the wall; she might even have deliberately hit him.

There are many factors which combine to make this sort of situation so difficult – the other person's behaviour, but also your own feelings, how you interpret the other person's motives and abilities, and the general context in which the event happens. You are going to think more about this by exploring the following case study.

Rosalie Williams

At Millstream Court where Marie works there are a number of young people who have multiple problems. Rosalie Williams is one such young woman. She has a hearing impairment, difficulties in communicating and severe learning disabilities, and is often aggressive to staff or other residents when things get too much for her.

During Marie's second week there was a staff meeting at which Rosalie was the main subject of discussion. It appeared that she had punched one of the support workers and broken her nose: the support worker was now off sick and there was a lot of sympathy for her. Many staff were angry and said that things had 'gone too far' this time. Some people were angry with Rosalie but others felt it wasn't really her fault because she gets very frustrated and has no other way of expressing herself. Some staff seemed to be directing their feelings at the management. They said they shouldn't have to work with someone like Rosalie and that Millstream Court isn't equipped to deal with people who are as 'severe' as she is. They wanted her to be removed. The manager's view was that Rosalie should be allowed to stay and there should be some extra support; and she had invited a psychologist along to discuss with staff how best to respond to what the psychologist called Rosalie's 'challenging behaviour'.

Marie didn't really know Rosalie but she felt a bit alarmed. Mostly, she just listened to the meeting and she noticed that Rosalie's key worker was undecided: he thought that if Rosalie was allowed to get away with this she would just do it again, but on the other hand he had worked hard to keep her in the unit for the last six months and he didn't want to give up yet.

3.1 Different ways of talking about difficult behaviour

Although the staff group came together to discuss how to respond to Rosalie's behaviour, you may have noticed that they approached it from very different perspectives. As the meeting progressed they used different words to describe the same situation. If you had been a fly on the wall, for the rest of the staff meeting you would have seen that they continued to describe the situation from very different viewpoints.

Different explanations for Rosalie's behaviour

Different people gave different explanations for why Rosalie had punched the support worker. One member of staff thought that Rosalie had lashed out because she was generally frustrated by her life. Another thought that Rosalie might not understand that it is not acceptable to hit people if you are unhappy. Someone else thought that Rosalie had been spoilt by her mother before she came to live at Millstream Court, so had never learned to control herself. Yet another thought that Rosalie has so few ways of communicating that she has to use violence. Another view was that Rosalie was simply seeking attention. The final member of staff thought that Rosalie should never have been placed with Millstream Court because it is not set up to deal with people with such severe needs as Rosalie has. This person thought that Rosalie was not getting the care she needs and this is why the situation escalated.

All these explanations are quite plausible and the sort of thing that any group of staff might have come up with. The different explanations lead logically to different strategies to prevent Rosalie from punching someone again.

Different ideas about how to respond to Rosalie

The person who thought that Rosalie was generally frustrated suggested a counselling service specifically designed for people with learning disabilities. The person who thought that Rosalie might not properly understand that she should not hit people suggested that they should do a more detailed assessment of her abilities and understanding, perhaps bringing in outside experts to help them do this. The member of staff who thought Rosalie's mother had spoiled her said it was really important that they treat her consistently and firmly so that she learns what behaviour is acceptable and what is not. The one who thought the violence was due to communication difficulties suggested that they tried to get Rosalie extra help with using sign language. The person who thought Rosalie was seeking attention said that they should simply ignore her when she behaved badly. The person who suggested Rosalie should never have been admitted to Millstream Court said that they should get her moved somewhere else.

You can see from this that how you understand a situation makes a difference to what you think should be done about it. The psychologist whom the manager of Millstream Court contacted used the term 'challenging behaviour' to describe Rosalie's outburst. This term has replaced older terms such as 'problem behaviour' or 'difficult behaviour'. This shift has been explained by Lowe and Felce (1995) as part of:

> … the general movement to use more respectful, less deficiency or problem-oriented language.

These authors go on to explain that it conveys:

> … something particular about how challenging behaviour should be viewed. The nature of the challenge was not a one-way affair but was a shared, or mutual, responsibility …

and they conclude that:

> The change in terminology served to point up the onus on services to understand and help the individual.

(Lowe and Felce, 1995, p. 118)

Calling Rosalie's behaviour 'challenging' is like saying, 'Rosalie isn't behaving badly; she's behaving in ways which are difficult for her care workers to manage. It's the service's responsibility to find ways of making things better.' This can include trying to change Rosalie's behaviour and the situations in which she is placed, as well as changing the way care workers respond to her.

When Marie had her interview for her job, the manager emphasised that staff at Millstream Court should treat the residents as 'normal' young people. But you might question whether the manager should be saying that the staff should treat residents 'as if they are normal'. If they do so, she and her colleagues have every right to feel angry and punitive towards Rosalie for hurting the support worker. Perhaps the manager should instead be saying something along the lines of: 'You are doing this job because Rosalie and people like her are different; they *can't* take the same responsibility as other people of their age. You need to take some of the responsibility that they can't manage on their own.'

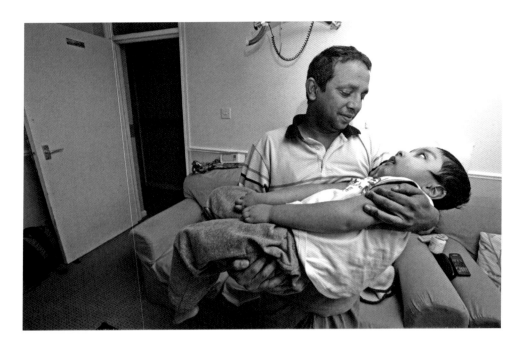

Taking responsibility according to individual difficulties

The same might be true of other service users, including those who tend to be more blamed than helped, such as young people who have been in trouble with the courts. They present different challenges but they also need to be approached with a respect for the difficulties that have led them to need a service in the first place. When such difficulties are compounded by discrimination and racism, people often find themselves on the receiving end of a 'double whammy' of personal difficulty and social disadvantage. If they then behave in challenging ways they are at even more risk of attracting a punitive approach from those who should be there to help and contain their behaviour.

3.3 Responding to challenging behaviour

What are the implications of describing something as 'challenging behaviour'? What does it mean about your understanding of what is going on, and how does it affect your response?

DVD

Activity 7   More about challenging behaviour

Allow about 30 minutes

In this activity you hear two people whose work involves dealing with this kind of situation.

Find Block 5, Unit 17, Activity 7 on the DVD.

Comment

So challenging behaviour achieves something for the person who does it. It doesn't occur without a reason. Carers often assume that if someone does something antisocial it is because they want attention. But there is nothing inherently wrong with seeking attention and it doesn't explain all behaviour. Sometimes people behave in challenging ways because they are in pain, or are hungry or thirsty, or are being asked to do something that is too difficult. Or they may not understand the concept of time, may be bored, or may have hearing problems or lack verbal communication.

It is important to rule out practical or ill-health reasons for someone's challenging behaviour. Lianne Bissell et al. report the case of a man with severe learning disabilities whose behaviour became much less violent when he had some dental problems fixed (Bissell et al., 2005). Of course you can't ever know for certain what has changed someone's behaviour. In this case, the staff had also changed how they responded to his violence and he was sleeping better. But it seems clear that getting the dental problems fixed helped, and it is important to remain alert to the possibility that challenging behaviour may be a response to health problems or other practical difficulties.

When people do not have much language, challenging behaviours can be a way of communicating, of making things happen, or stopping things from happening. Most behaviours are partly learned and they usually achieve something for the person concerned. People may resort to challenging behaviour because they want you to go away or stop making demands on them. Not only are these ideas helpful in relation to people with learning disabilities but they can be applied equally to truancy, problem drinking, and so on.

Finding the 'function' of a behaviour – in other words what it does for the person in that particular setting or relationship – is an important first step in helping the person to change it. A psychologist such as Anthea Sperlinger in the audio recording would usually start by asking staff to observe and record Rosalie's behaviour and to note any other times when she gets aggressive. They might use a form called an ABC chart, which notes what happened before an outburst (the antecedent – A), what happened during the incident (the behaviour – B), and then what happened afterwards (the consequence – C). Aggression does not always mean the same thing. For Rosalie it may be the only way she knows of saying 'stop' or controlling what happens around her; for someone else it might be the way they get staff to take notice of them or to take them to their room.

Once an assessment has focused on what the behaviour is *for*, staff can figure out how to deal with it. Anthea uses the phrase 'very vigilant and good detectives' to describe the staff's role: they have to stand back from the immediate situation and not react personally. In this case, if you could watch a video recording of the incident, you would see that the support worker had just asked Rosalie to sort some cards – something which was too difficult for her – so she lashed out because she couldn't do the task she had been set. This is not attention-seeking behaviour: quite the opposite, it is called 'demand avoidance'. If Rosalie is taught a new sign for saying 'stop and go away', and all the staff know that when she uses it they must act accordingly, she may not need to be aggressive in the future. At the moment the staff are not alert to Rosalie's attempts to signal when she wants to bring activities to an end. They don't all use Makaton (a signing system specifically for people with learning disabilities) or receive training in communication skills, so they also need to learn some new behaviours!

If you start from the point of view that a person's behaviour does have a function and is a form of communication, you can try to avoid the stresses that lead to difficulties. For example, you can make sure that you present activities which are right for them, and you can provide enough of the right kind of support. It means that you don't just shrug your shoulders and keep out of the way of someone like Rosalie, or blame and punish her. Instead, you recognise that she isn't *choosing* not to learn or to behave badly – she just can't operate at this level of difficulty.

3.4 Safeguards in behaviour programmes

Behaviour programmes seek to build on a person's ways of controlling their environment. They focus on building service users' skills and helping them to develop alternatives to unacceptable behaviour which work for them. But planning in detail how to react to someone is a far cry from most everyday relationships, which is why we are considering it in this unit. It could even be seen as quite manipulative or controlling.

Should anyone consciously shape the behaviour of others by rewarding some behaviours and communication and not others? Are we all shaping people's behaviours anyway by what we do and say, even if we haven't thought about it and it just happens in a haphazard way? Is the situation different when dealing with people like Rosalie who have difficulty learning from the jumble of responses they usually come up against? The way behaviour programmes are justified is to say that, because the situation falls outside 'normal' social expectations, a new set of rules is needed.

Chad Botley, whom you heard on the DVD, stressed the need for staff to have a clear set of values and access to multidisciplinary input when dealing with challenging behaviour. He identified the risk that 'staff might tip over and respond physically instead of verbally in difficult or aggressive situations' and he also emphasised that structures should be available to 'provide a framework within which staff can feel safe to express their views and concerns'. Anthea Sperlinger also talked about the need for staff to feel supported and 'contained' if they are to be able to cope with challenging behaviour. If staff are not appropriately supported they can end up providing unsafe, inadequate or abusive care to people who have challenging behaviour.

Activity 8 Rules for managing difficult behaviour
Allow about 15 minutes

Imagine you are a member of staff who is being asked to respond to Rosalie in a particular way, which has been set out in a written behaviour programme. See if you can come up with a list of rules that you would feel comfortable with, to guide you and your colleagues when following the programme.

Comment

My rules would include the following.

- First of all, check that Rosalie's health and care needs are being met and have not changed.

- We should have a properly qualified psychologist to help us work out what is best and then discuss the programme together so that we all know how to put it into practice.

- The behaviour we are trying to 'treat' should be something that Rosalie could change, not something like seizures, which are always going to be out of her control.

- We should be helping her to manage things better for herself in future, not just taking something away from her.

- We should be aiming to help her do things she wants to do and opening up opportunities for her.

- We should try to provide opportunities for her to give as well as receive.

- We should find a way of working with her which keeps us and other residents safe.

- We shouldn't do anything against the law.

- We shouldn't damage her or hurt her. For example, I would not be willing to hit her, although I would hold her down to stop her hurting herself or someone else, if I had been shown how to do this properly and if other non-physical techniques had not worked.

- We shouldn't give her medication just to make life easier for us.

Some agencies have developed codes of practice to formalise rules such as these. However, even where proper programmes are in place emergencies may arise. These often call for a quick response to cool someone down or to remove others from harm. Excessive force might easily be applied in such situations unless staff are given help in anticipating and dealing with emergencies. You might remember Chad Botley talking about training staff in ways to intervene early in a situation that might escalate, and using the gentlest forms of physical contact first, such as holding someone's arm. This is particularly important because care workers may be frightened or at risk themselves. This is an area of practice which needs particular attention in guidelines and is often dealt with under the title of 'control and restraint' or 'physical interventions'. As a general principle 'reasonable' force in such situations involves the *minimum* needed to calm the person down. A model national policy (Harris et al., 1996, 2008) advocates the notion of a 'gradient of control' whereby:

> … when staff respond with [any] physical intervention, they follow a predetermined sequence which begins with the application of the least restrictive options and gradually increases the level of restriction. The sequence is terminated as soon as control is established over the person's behaviour.

(Harris et al., 1996, p. 35)

Rules, policies and guidelines are particularly important if force is used, in order to make sure that responses to challenging behaviour do not become abusive or unsafe.

Force should be used only if it is absolutely necessary and as a last resort. Once care workers start using any degree of physical force there is a danger of it being used too readily or too harshly. Staff can become used to the idea that they can use force on service users, and workplaces can build up cultures in which unsafe and harmful care is provided. In the final section of this unit, you will explore how these workplace cultures can lead to poor-quality care.

Key points

- How you describe a person's behaviour will affect how you respond to it.

- The term 'challenging behaviour' has been introduced to shift responsibility for difficult behaviour from the service user to the service provider.

- A key way of managing difficult behaviour is to work out its *function*: in other words what it achieves for that person in that particular setting or situation. Behaviour programmes can then aim to expand a person's skills and opportunities, to enable them to fulfil the same function in a less disruptive way.

4 Unacceptable practice in workplaces

You have seen how care can go wrong in specific cases, for example when a care worker such as Marie has not been adequately trained for intimate care tasks, or when working with a service user like Rosalie presents challenges for which staff have not developed adequate strategies. But poor care practice does not arise solely from the actions and needs of individuals; it can be embedded in the ethos and habits of workplaces.

In the case of Rosalie, you read how staff at Millstream Court met to discuss the incident of the broken nose and weigh up what ought to happen. It seems that this was an environment in which a lot of thought was put into providing the right care for a challenging resident like Rosalie. By contrast, in Unit 15 you read about the bedrooms of the Cedar Court nursing home (Chapter 14 in the Reader), another environment where care work was challenging, but where little thought seemed to be given to residents' needs, and where poor practice was routine.

Meeting residents' needs?

4.1 When does unacceptable care become abusive?

To help you focus on the experience of living in Cedar Court, read about a fictional resident in the case study below.

Living in Cedar Court

Alan Harris is 86 and has been a resident of Cedar Court for a year, following a stroke. His mobility is very restricted and his speech impaired. His memory had already been poor and after the stroke it worsened, so that he gets confused about where he is and who the staff are. He does not want to be in a nursing home and becomes very angry at times – shouting at staff and hitting out when they start 'doing things' to him. However, at other times he is calm. He usually enjoys being in the lounge among other people.

In his earlier life Alan was married, had three children, worked as an electrician and spent a lot of his leisure time coaching a youth football team, as well as being generally active in the community. Two years ago his wife died. Owing to his poor memory, he found living on his own a struggle. For a few months he lived with the younger of his two daughters until he had the stroke. He believes he ought to be looked after at home by one of his children.

Because of his outbursts the nursing auxiliaries call him Victor (after Victor Meldrew in the television programme *One Foot in the Grave*). He is also one of the 'buzzers', who frequently press the buzzer for attention and whose bed gets moved away from the wall so that he can't reach it. The auxiliaries often have difficulty wiping, washing and dressing him. One night when he kept shouting, two auxiliaries shut him in the toilet until he stopped.

Reader

Activity 9 How bad is the practice in the Cedar Court bedrooms?

Allow about 20 minutes

Turn to Chapter 14, 'Bedroom abuse: the hidden work in a nursing home', by Geraldine Lee-Treweek' in the Reader (pages 107–11) and skim through it again, looking for information relevant to the questions below.

(a) Try to imagine Alan's experiences during his nights and mornings at Cedar Court. Why do you think he gets angry at times?

(b) According to Lee-Treweek's account, what do the auxiliaries do that amounts to mistreatment of residents?

Comment

(a) I imagined Alan having long boring spells awake in the dark, wondering where he is and how long it is until morning – wanting to ask someone but not being able to reach the buzzer – and feeling angry that he seems to have been abandoned by the world and can't do anything about it. Then dozing and being suddenly wakened by strangers messing about with his bedclothes and leg bag. Then waking again in the morning to find he is once again not in his own home, not with family or friends but with strangers coming to do things to him – giving him food he didn't choose, dressing him in clothes he didn't choose – and saying patronising things, then moving away when he tries to speak. I imagined any of these things making him angry when his thoughts focus on them.

(b) Lee-Treweek says that auxiliaries treat the residents as 'objects' rather than people – bodies to be serviced. She says they ignore residents' spatial rights and instead move freely and casually around residents' bedrooms and around their bodies without asking permission. They don't say 'hello' when they come in or 'goodbye' when they leave. They talk with each other about residents and often ignore them when they speak, acting as though the residents are not present. All of this has the effect of 'depersonalising' the residents. When residents are 'disorderly' the auxiliaries adopt a 'hard' approach, restraining them and telling them off. If residents resist this, the auxiliaries 'punish' them by avoiding them or making fun of them.

Clearly, there is much about the experience of someone in Alan's circumstances that is likely to be upsetting, but how much of that upset should be 'blamed' on the auxiliaries? They have a difficult job to do. If 'depersonalising' residents is a strategy that helps auxiliaries to work quickly and efficiently and cope with some very challenging situations, is it such a bad thing? In the next part of the case study, you will read how this depersonalisation feels to someone like Alan.

Experiencing depersonalisation

Alan has had an active life as husband, father, electrician and well-known figure in the local community. He got involved, he got things done and people respected him. Now he finds himself dependent on people who know nothing of all that and pay attention only to what he can't do. As well as losing a lot of physical capability because of his illness, he has lost the social strength of being part of a community of people he could rely on because of their ties to him. Being treated as a 'non-person' exaggerates his sense of helplessness. He is afraid that he will be unable to draw attention to his own particular needs because he is nobody in particular. People don't take notice when he speaks. He is just given what all the other residents get. He feels very unimportant.

Often he feels lonely, helpless and anxious. Apart from a visit once or twice a week from one or other of his children, he has little contact with the world outside Cedar Court. So, with his failing memory, he is losing confidence in his own views about the world and his place in it. He knows he disagrees with a lot of what the auxiliary nurses do and say, but when he tries to complain he can't get his thoughts together and ends up just getting frustrated and angry. Sometimes the auxiliaries respond by making fun of him, which makes him feel humiliated and despairing.

The auxiliaries focus only on 'servicing' residents' bodies, yet many of the residents will be like our fictional resident, Alan, with wide-ranging needs. Like him they will be trying to cope with the loss of family life and life in their local community and at the same time experiencing significant losses of physical and mental powers. Yet at this time when they need support and comfort they find themselves treated as non-persons. The main place where they spend time – the bedrooms – is 'colonised' by the auxiliaries, as Lee-Treweek puts it. The auxiliaries treat it as their space, where their values and priorities take precedence and what they say goes. So, instead of residents being supported in coming to terms with the losses and upheavals in their lives, they are left feeling worthless and purposeless. What the auxiliaries might see as a briskly efficient approach to getting their work done may have a profoundly undermining effect on residents.

Does depersonalising residents, taking a 'hard' approach and 'punishing' and humiliating them amount to abuse? Lee-Treweek reports that the auxiliaries thought that physical abuse was unacceptable, but suggests that they engaged in mental and emotional cruelty. What exactly counts as abuse? In 2000 the UK government published guidance on protecting vulnerable adults from abuse in a document called *No Secrets*. It provides a definition of abuse and identifies six main types of abuse.

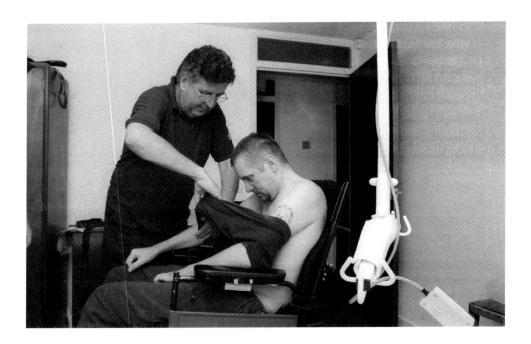

Caring or getting the
work done?

Extracts from *No Secrets*

Abuse is a violation of an individual's human and civil rights by any other
person or persons.

[...]

Abuse may consist of a single act or repeated acts. It may be physical,
verbal or psychological, it may be an act of neglect or an omission to act,
or it may occur when a vulnerable person is persuaded to enter into a
financial or sexual transaction to which he or she has not consented, or
cannot consent. Abuse can occur in any relationship and may result in
significant harm to, or exploitation of, the person subjected to it.

A consensus has emerged identifying the following main different forms
of abuse:

- *physical abuse*, including hitting, slapping, pushing, kicking, misuse
  of medication, restraint, or inappropriate sanctions;

- *sexual abuse*, including rape and sexual assault or sexual acts to
  which the vulnerable adult has not consented, or could not consent
  or was pressured into consenting;

- *psychological abuse*, including emotional abuse, threats of harm
  or abandonment, deprivation of contact, humiliation, blaming,
  controlling, intimidation, coercion, harassment, verbal abuse, isola-
  tion or withdrawal from services or
  supportive networks;

- *financial or material abuse*, including theft, fraud, exploitation,
  pressure in connection with wills, property or inheritance or financial
  transactions, or the misuse or misappropriation of property,
  possessions or benefits;

- *neglect and acts of omission*, including ignoring medical or physical care needs, failure to provide access to appropriate health, social care or educational services, the withholding of the necessities of life, such as medication, adequate nutrition and heating; and

- *discriminatory abuse*, including racist, sexist, that based on a person's disability, and other forms of harassment, slurs or similar treatment.

Any or all of these types of abuse may be perpetrated as the result of deliberate intent, negligence or ignorance.

(Source: DH, 2000, pp. 8–9)

Activity 10   Is what happens in Cedar Court bedrooms abuse?

Allow about 15 minutes

Chapter 14 in the Reader about Cedar Court is titled 'Bedroom abuse'. Do you think that what the auxiliaries do amounts to abuse?

Read back through the *No Secrets* definition of abuse in the box above and highlight anything that applies to the actions of the Cedar Court auxiliaries. Then make your own judgement as to whether what goes on in the Cedar Court bedrooms should be described as abuse.

Comment

I highlighted many of the words under the heading *psychological abuse*. The Cedar Court chapter certainly gives examples of humiliation, coercion, verbal abuse, deprivation of contact and withdrawal of services, and most of the other items are also indicated in one way or another.

There also seemed to be evidence of *neglect*; for example, residents were left unable to reach their buzzers and their needs were ignored. Also there were jokes based on residents' disabilities, which is *discriminatory* abuse.

And in spite of the auxiliaries' stated disapproval of *physical abuse*, it did seem that there was potential misuse of restraint and also inappropriate sanctions.

Cedar Court residents will, like Alan, have played active roles in society and been used to enjoying 'human and civil rights', but now find themselves denied these rights by the auxiliaries, the rulers of the 'bedroom world'. Using the *No Secrets* guidelines, it seems clear that there is evidence of abuse in the Cedar Court bedrooms.

Although the Cedar Court auxiliaries might think of themselves as good workers, getting on with a difficult job, the practices they have developed are not acceptable. They may be efficient practices but they are also abusive.

4.2 How unacceptable practice develops

How does bad practice develop? Is it that the wrong people are recruited, or is it something about the environment in which they work? You met a fictional resident of Cedar Court in the previous section; here is a description of a fictional nursing auxiliary.

Working in the bedrooms of Cedar Court

Lauren Stewart has been a nursing auxiliary at Cedar Court for two years. She found the work extremely hard to begin with. Residents were very difficult, sometimes shouting aggressively and hitting out, which made her feel intimidated and anxious. She also found the shifts very tiring, with a lot of physical activity and many residents to get round. She isn't sure how she would have got through her first few shifts if she hadn't been befriended by Tara Wilkinson, one of the other auxiliaries, who showed her what to do and helped her out. At first Lauren thought she wasn't up to the job, but now she takes pride in being good at this difficult but important work. She always wanted to work with people and she likes the camaraderie among her colleagues.

One resident who is often a source of trouble is 'Victor'. He is always asking for things and complaining. He sometimes gets angry and starts shouting, which is upsetting to other residents. He even hits out at people with his stick. Tara showed Lauren how to handle people like Victor. She said, 'Take no nonsense – give as good as you get.' Tara can just bustle Victor through his wash and into his clothes, ignoring his struggles and keeping up a stream of witty responses to his shouting. Recently, Victor accused the two of them of stealing his clothes when Tara put on his hat and coat and paraded round saying, 'Paris catwalk – it's the Victor Meldrew collection. Who could resist it?' Lauren couldn't help giggling. Tara knows how to stay a step ahead of Victor and his tantrums. She doesn't let him upset their busy schedule.

Activity 11   Failing to respond to need
Allow about 15 minutes

Alan (Victor) is at Cedar Court because he needs a lot of support. As well as his mental and physical needs, he is also struggling to come to terms with the loss of the life and people he knew. Lauren is employed to provide care for residents like Alan. Why does she not respond to his need for support? Jot down some ideas.

Comment

Here are my thoughts:

- Lauren sees Victor as a 'problem', not as someone who needs help. She thinks about how to manage him rather than how to help him. She is concerned about how to 'contain' his aggression, rather than how to understand it and address its causes. She doesn't even think of him as the person 'Alan'.

- She sees the purpose of her job as to create order out of the disorder in the Cedar Court bedrooms – the physical mess, the spitting, sobbing, confusion and aggression. Her priority is to produce presentable residents within a tight time schedule. She doesn't feel she has time to spare for chatting with residents. Consequently, she knows very little about Alan, his life and his needs.

- She has been given no instruction or training to lead her to think differently. She does the work in the same way that others around her do it. She learned the job from them and now she shares the beliefs, values and practices of their subculture. As far as she can see, they all do a difficult job as well as it can be done.

As the Cedar Court bedroom world shows, bad practice is often less a matter of care workers being 'bad' in themselves than of a work environment which tolerates, or even encourages, bad practice. In an environment where:

- workloads allow little time for caring relationships with individuals

- a care worker's performance is judged in terms of efficiency rather than empathy and support

- there is little training or supervision

the conditions are right for poor practice to flourish.

Also, as you read in Unit 15, when people live and work in an enclosed environment and when there are clear-cut boundaries between the more powerful and the less powerful, repressive regimes spring up very easily. An 'institutional perspective' develops – a point of view which takes for granted the priorities and interests of the powerful and redefines the interests of the weak to fit in. From this institutional perspective the powerful come to be seen as virtuous and the weak as wayward and needing firm discipline. This leads to the idea that 'punishment' is sometimes necessary. Yet punishment is not normally a concept that plays a part in relationships between adults. In everyday life people generally relate to each other as equal citizens, whereas punishment implies a relationship of non-consensual authority and subordination. When Lee-Treweek writes about the Cedar Court auxiliaries 'Telling people off … and "teaching them a lesson"' (Reader, Chapter 14, p. 110) she is signalling a regime which is humiliating to residents because it positions them not as adult citizens but as badly behaved members of a lower order.

Am I being a bit harsh on Lauren and her colleagues? Might not punishment be appropriate occasionally, when a resident like Alan is particularly aggressive? What else can Lauren do? The answer is – a lot. You have already seen that thinking of aggression as 'challenging behaviour' makes a difference to how you respond to it. It makes you think about why the person is behaving in the way they are, and what can be done to prevent them getting into such a state in the first place. This is the sort of approach that is set out in, for example, the UK National Occupational Standards (NOS) for Health and Social Care. This encourages a very different environment and very different relationships. Instead of allowing a gulf to develop between care workers and service users, and a power hierarchy to become entrenched, it advocates open communications, equality and trust.

National Occupational Standards for Health and Social Care

HSC336a: Contribute to preventing abusive and aggressive behaviour

[...]

You need to show that,

1   you communicate with others in a manner which:

   - is appropriate to them

   - encourages an open exchange of views and information

   - minimises any constraints to communication

   - is free from discrimination and oppression

   - acknowledges the rights of everyone present and is supportive of those rights.

2   you maintain the environment in a way which encourages meaningful interactions

3   you take actions to maintain calmness and safety in a manner which minimises any restriction of movement and which does not deny people's rights

4   you take appropriate action to prevent triggers to **abusive or aggressive behaviour** occurring and to enable individuals to find alternative ways of expressing their feelings

5   you protect potential victims at whom the behaviour may be directed.

(Source: Skills for Care, 2005, Section HSC336a)

Activity 12   Managing aggressive behaviour

Allow about 10 minutes

Read back through the list in the NOS box, thinking about Lauren's response to Alan's aggressive outbursts. Tick the things in the list that you think she does and put a cross against those she doesn't do.

Comment

I had no ticks and I had crosses against nearly all the list items. On one or two points I felt that Lee-Treweek didn't give us quite enough evidence to make a judgement, but generally it is clear that the approach taken by Lauren and the other auxiliaries is more or less the opposite of the one outlined in the NOS. And if the NOS approach is correct, then the implication is that the auxiliaries' approach, far from controlling aggressive behaviour, is actually making it worse. They are creating conditions that are likely to stimulate aggressive behaviour.

The contrast between repressive and open regimes is brought out very clearly if you compare the relationship between Lauren and Alan with the relationship you observed in the kitchen at Seven Oaks between Wendy Miller and Tony Connor in Unit 16.

Activity 13 Comparing repressive relationships with open ones
Allow about 10 minutes

Think back to your visit to Seven Oaks for Activity 4 of Unit 16: to the scene in the kitchen where Tony Connor and Wendy Miller were cooking and chatting together.

(a) Go back again to items 1 and 2 of the list in the box above, but this time think about Wendy's relationship with Tony. Using a different coloured pen, tick the things you think Wendy does and put a cross against those she doesn't do. (Note that the scene doesn't really provide direct evidence on items 3, 4 and 5.)

(b) Compare Tony's experience of his relationship with Wendy and Alan's experience of his relationship with Lauren. Write down the main ways in which Tony's experience differs.

Comment

(a) This time I ticked everything for items 1 and 2 in the box. Working alongside each other in the kitchen enabled Tony and Wendy to have meaningful interactions. Wendy's talk is not focused on supervising Tony and telling him to do things. She is conversing person to person – treating his concerns as being as important as hers. Consequently, she knows about Tony's past life.

(b) Because Tony is allowed to get on with his cooking, he has an opportunity to express the personality he developed in his working life. He is treated not as a 'problem' to be managed but as a fellow worker. Attention is not drawn to what he can't do. He doesn't have other people talking about him as though he isn't there. He doesn't have jokes made about what he says and does. He isn't confronted or contradicted. He is accepted as he is. Far from making him feel dependent, depersonalised and devalued, his relationship with Wendy enables him to experience being a useful, interesting, valued person.

We do not learn whether Tony ever behaves aggressively, but it certainly appears that he has a lot less reason to do so at Seven Oaks than Alan has at Cedar Court. Because of the way Lauren sees her job and the way she relates to Alan she greatly increases the frustration and loneliness of his life. Far from thinking of him as the person 'Alan', she thinks of him as 'Victor', the cantankerous figure of fun. To her this may be just harmless humour, but it makes her insensitive to Alan's needs and reinforces his sense of being abandoned in an unsympathetic world.

Within a regime like the Cedar Court 'bedroom world' a cycle can set in where insensitive practice triggers aggressive behaviour, which then brings an uncompromising response from care workers, giving rise to yet more aggression from residents. Regular repetitions of this cycle then appear to justify the 'hard' subculture within which a 'no-nonsense approach' seems normal and punishment seems just a natural part of the routine. To break this self-reinforcing cycle

requires intervention from outside. But that requires knowledge of what is going
on to reach the world outside. One way for that to happen is for a care worker to
recognise bad practice for what it is and report it.

4.3 Reporting unacceptable practice

How might a care worker identify bad practice and how might it be reported?
The next section of our story explores this.

Tara goes too far

One day when Lauren took Victor to the lounge, one of the trained staff
there told her about his past youth work in his local community and that he
had received an OBE. After that Lauren began to think differently about him
and felt uncomfortable with her friend's jokes. When, a few days later, Tara
told her how she and another auxiliary had shut Victor in the toilet to stop
him shouting, Lauren said she didn't think it was right. Tara just laughed.
Afterwards, Lauren wondered whether she should do something. She could
see that things weren't likely to get better for Alan unless she did. Should
she report the incident? She did think that Tara had gone too far but she
wasn't sure whether the incident was serious enough to report, or whom
she should report it to. She was also unsure what would happen to Tara and
what, indeed, might happen to herself. Would the other auxiliaries find out?
Would she be able to continue working with them? She had seen stories
in the news about 'whistleblowers'. Would she be a whistleblower if she
reported Tara – and what would the implications of that be?

Activity 14   Should bad practice be reported?

Allow about 15 minutes

Write down your thoughts on the following three questions.

(a) Should Lauren report the incident with Tara and Alan?

(b) If so, whom should she report it to and how?

(c) What is likely to happen if she does report the incident?

Comment

(a) If Lauren were a registered social care worker, as opposed to a nursing
auxiliary, she would have clear duties under the Code of Practice for Social
Care Workers published by the General Social Care Council (2002). (There
is no exactly equivalent general code covering health care assistants at the
time of writing (2008), although, as noted in Unit 4, Section 1.2, there are
specific codes covering various aspects of health care practice. However,
the same general principles would apply to Lauren.) On the question of
whether to report the incident, as you can see in the box that follows, item 3.2
requires social care workers 'to challenge and report dangerous, abusive,
discriminatory or exploitative behaviour and practice'. Also, item 3.5 requires
them to report 'where the practice of colleagues may be unsafe or adversely

affecting standards of care'. If Lauren has concerns about the effect on Alan of Tara's actions, then it is her responsibility to report them, even if she does not have a formal legal duty to do so.

Code of Practice for Social Care Workers

3   As a social care worker, you must promote the independence of service users while protecting them as far as possible from danger or harm.

This includes:

[...]

3.2 Using established processes and procedures to challenge and report dangerous, abusive, discriminatory or exploitative behaviour and practice;

[...]

3.5 Informing your employer or an appropriate authority where the practice of colleagues may be unsafe or adversely affecting standards of care; ...

(Source: General Social Care Council, 2002, p. 15)

(b) Regarding whom to report to, the code indicates that Lauren should inform her employer or an appropriate authority, and that she should use 'established processes and procedures to challenge and report'. Basically, she should normally report to her manager in the first instance. According to Lee-Treweek 'many [auxiliaries] gave accounts of whistleblowing on violent colleagues in the past' (Reader, p. 110), so it seems that there is an established procedure which Lauren can follow – although in the past it has been used only to report physical abuse rather than emotional abuse.

(c) As to what will happen if Lauren reports the incident, ideally there will be a well-established procedure whereby the issue is taken up with Tara and resolved, as appropriate, through a warning, disciplinary action, further training, or even dismissal. Meanwhile, Lauren ought to be able to continue with her work without consequences. However, this ideal has not always been achieved.

Unfortunately, institutions have not always responded appropriately to concerns raised by employees. Instead of addressing the concerns, some employers have turned on the whistleblowers and disciplined or even dismissed them, as the newspaper story below shows.

As this story reveals, care workers who draw attention to bad practice can find themselves vulnerable to reprisals from employers even, as in this case, when six are acting together. If none of the other auxiliaries at Cedar Court is prepared to back Lauren up and if the management are unsympathetic, she may find herself in a difficult position. However, the story above also shows that there is legal protection for care workers who report bad practice. 'The case was due to be heard in three weeks' time but the West Yorkshire council opted for an ... out-of-court settlement.' (*Daily Mail*, 2007).

Six care workers sacked for whistleblowing awarded £1m

Daily Mail 14 August 2007
www.dailymail.co.uk/pages/live/articles/news/news.html?
in_article_id=475310&in_page_id=1770

Six whistleblowing care workers sacked for lifting the lid on
a shocking catalogue of mismanagement in childrens' homes
have won a one million pound payout.
The intrepid sextet spoke out after witnessing serious failings
which were damaging the lives of vulnerable youngsters.
Karen Allcock, Keith Bayliss, Clive Womersley, Vincent
Felix, Doug Lafferty and Grant Morley were sacked in
February 2006 – just a month after revealing how children
in care were being treated by Wakefield Council.

The six successful whistleblowers

The Public Interest Disclosure Act 1998 is designed to protect whistleblowers
from victimisation:

> The Public Interest Disclosure Act is popularly known as the whistleblowing
> law. It forms part of employment legislation and protects employees and
> other workers from reprisals for public interest whistleblowing.

(Public Concern at Work, undated)

Activity 15   What does the Public Interest Disclosure Act cover?
Allow about 20 minutes

When you want to know more about laws that apply to health and social care,
you have a very handy resource in the HSC Resource Bank.

Log on to the course website and follow the link to the HSC Resource Bank.
Then search for the Public Interest Disclosure Act. Browse through the pages
about the Act, looking for anything relevant to Lauren's case, and try to decide
whether Lauren is protected by the Act.

Comment

The main relevant points are:

- Lauren's 'disclosure' is 'in good faith'.
- The disclosure 'tends to show … that the health or safety of … [an] individual
  has been … endangered'.
- She may disclose to her employer, or to someone else if she 'does not make
  the disclosure for personal gain', and she 'reasonably believes that … she
  will be subject to a detriment by making the disclosure'.

This law does not specifically mention 'abuse'. Instead it refers to endangering
'health or safety'. While it can be claimed that shutting Alan in the toilet did

endanger his health (including his mental health) and his safety, what Lauren was most concerned about was the humiliation and sense of helplessness and abandonment that Alan experienced. This 'emotional abuse' is not directly specified in the Act, so she will be better protected if she focuses on the health and safety aspect.

UNISON, the union representing the interests of care workers, has welcomed the growth in efforts to protect care workers from victimisation, but has warned that are still grounds for concern:

> … despite strictures by ministers about openness, local whistleblowing policies, clinical governance and the Public Interest Disclosure Act, there is still a climate of secrecy and intimidation in many organisations, making it more difficult to flag up concerns about the duties of care or the public interest.

(UNISON, 2003, p. 9)

Many employers, however, now say that they take reports of abuse very seriously and that they do not victimise whistleblowers, but act promptly and responsibly to address the practice they report. That is what the employers claimed in the following case.

Whistleblower accuses staff of 'appalling' abuse at care home

[…]

The most shocking allegations levelled against the home include:

- a 35-year-old man strapped to his wheelchair for hours each day so that he almost lost his ability to walk and suffered damage to his feet as he struggled to get free;

- a man given his daily medication while strapped to the toilet and crying;

- improper medication procedures for people in care, risking overdose;

- adults left caked in their own excrement for hours during the night.

The allegations will highlight growing concerns over how people with severe learning disabilities are looked after in homes …

… the whistleblower was a senior support worker who had worked for [the organisation] for 19 months. He raised his concerns last year, prompting an investigation by the company and Hertfordshire County Council.

[…]

The whistleblower claims some staff regularly fabricated records to show they had taken individuals on leisure activities such as walks, swimming or to a disco. In reality, he claims, most were kept in the home while the staff watched television.

[…]

'It became clear that my son's standard of care had fallen far below any acceptable standard,' [one resident's father] said. 'An institutionalised culture of neglect appears to have developed over the years. It is all too easy to mistreat people who are not able to stand up for themselves.'

[…]

[The employing organisation claimed that] 'The allegations came to light as part of [our] whistleblowing process and were taken very seriously. An experienced manager was brought in to carry out a full investigation, and a comprehensive report, which detailed actions to be taken, was produced.

'All these actions have now been put in place, including providing additional staff and management support at the service. All issues have now been dealt with and best practice is being observed at the service. Ensuring the wellbeing of all the people we support is our top priority at all times.'

(Source: Barnett, 2006)

If Lauren is worried about the risks of getting involved in all this, she can seek advice. For example, UNISON's handbook *Duty of Care* is:

> … designed to give practical guidance to health service staff at all levels and in situations where there may be a conflict between:

> - what their employer expects them to do

> and

> - what they believe is in the best interests of patients, the health of colleagues or themselves, or the wider public interest.

(UNISON, 2003, p. 2)

Alternatively, Lauren could contact the charity Action on Elder Abuse, by phoning its helpline 'Elder Abuse Response'. Here is a quotation from their leaflet:

> 'It was really difficult telling on my colleague who was making old people in our care miserable, but the helpline gave me lots of support. I'm glad I did it.'

(Action on Elder Abuse, 2001)

Reporting bad practice is not an easy step to take, but it is one of the responsibilities of a care worker.

4.4 Preventing unacceptable practice

To rely on good intentions and common sense is not enough in care environments. Care service users can easily find themselves in the position of depending on somebody for support and not having any easy way of commenting on, let alone complaining about, the way that person treats them. This is all the more so if the service user has learning disabilities or difficulty in communicating. Consequently, it is essential that steps are taken to guard against bad practice, particularly when so much of care practice is hidden from public view, with all the attendant dangers you have been reading about.

Often bad practice occurs because well-intentioned staff are inadequately trained, not given clear guidelines and not supervised effectively. But sometimes it may arise because of the tendency of particular individuals to bullying or punitive behaviour. Either way safeguards are needed and these are the responsibility of all organisations that provide care. The next box contains some extracts from a code of practice for employers of social care workers published by The General Social Care Council (GSCC).

Code of Practice for Employers of Social Care Workers

1 As a social care employer, you must: …

1.1 [use] rigorous and thorough recruitment and selection processes focused on making sure that only people who have the appropriate knowledge and skills and who are suitable to provide social care are allowed to enter your workforce;

[…]

2 As a social care employer, you must have written policies and procedures in place to enable social care workers to meet the GSCC's Code of Practice for Social Care Workers.

This includes:

[…]

2.2 Effectively managing and supervising staff to support effective practice and good conduct and supporting staff to address deficiencies in their performance;

[…]

3 As a social care employer, you must provide …

3.1 induction, training and development opportunities to help social care workers do their jobs effectively and prepare for new and changing roles and responsibilities;

[…]

4 As a social care employer, you must put into place and implement written policies and procedures to deal with dangerous, discriminatory or exploitative behaviour and practice.

This includes:

4.1 Making it clear to social care workers that bullying, harassment or any form of unjustifiable discrimination is not acceptable and taking action to deal with such behaviour;

4.2 Establishing and promoting procedures for social care workers to report dangerous, discriminatory, abusive or exploitative behaviour and practice and dealing with these reports promptly, effectively and openly;

4.3 Making it clear to social care workers, service users and carers that violence, threats or abuse to staff are not acceptable and having clear policies and procedures for minimising the risk of violence and managing violent incidents; …

(Source: General Social Care Council, 2002, pp. 6–8)

Activity 16   What safeguards are needed at Cedar Court?

Allow about 15 minutes

Read back through the extracts in the box above, this time thinking about what you know of Cedar Court.

(a) Put one star against any paragraph you think is likely to need attention in the case of Cedar Court.

(b) Put two stars against paragraphs you think definitely need attention.

(c) Put three stars against paragraphs you think need very urgent attention.

Comment

My answers are as follows:

(a) I put one star against paragraph 1.1, as we are not told much about the recruitment policy, but it probably needs checking.

(b) I put two stars against paragraph 2, as we are given no hint that the auxiliaries are aware of written policies, so it seems quite possible that none exists.

(c) I put three stars against all the rest, because the evidence from Lee-Treweek's article implies that in each of these areas there are major shortcomings which are leading directly to unacceptable practice.

As you can see, there is much that a care-providing organisation can do to protect service users by trying to eliminate the conditions in which bad practice develops. In the rest of Block 5 you will be exploring in more detail how this can be done.

Key points

- Unacceptable care practice is only partly about badly performed care tasks; it is also to do with undermining people emotionally by failing to relate to them as people, making them feel depersonalised and worthless.

- In care work, bad practice is often not to do with individual care workers but rather with care environments where inappropriate attitudes, beliefs and practices develop over time and become taken for granted.

- Reporting bad practice is a duty of care workers, but it is not easy. Care workers have some protection in law and can seek advice if they want it.

- Care employers are responsible for taking steps to ensure that they provide safeguards against bad practice.

Conclusion

In this unit you have looked at some of the reasons why poor-quality, unsafe and even abusive care can occur. Some reasons are at the level of the management and organisation of services, such as poor induction and training for new staff. You may not be involved in the management and organisation of services at the moment, but, if not now, you may be in the future. If you are a care worker you might become a manager; if you are a service user or an informal carer you might become a trustee of a voluntary organisation which provides care services. People working at this level have considerable power to influence the safety and quality of care.

Care workers and social workers can also take responsibility for some of the ways in which care can be made high-quality and safe.

- Informal carers and care workers can try to imagine what it is like for a particular person to receive care. They can ask them how they would like their care to be delivered and be mindful of their privacy and dignity.

- Service users can try to be clear and assertive about what they want and can empower themselves by getting support from other people in similar situations and formal support groups.

- Care workers can acknowledge when they are not properly prepared for a task and take responsibility for their own training.

- Informal carers and care workers can think about the implications of how they describe behaviour that they find difficult. They can try to understand why the person might be behaving in a challenging manner, and not just assume that they are 'attention seeking' or 'difficult'.

- Staff who find themselves in a workplace where poor care has become routine can try to raise the issues with their line manager or beyond.

Care workers are very rarely solely responsible for making care safe and of good quality – they are nearly always operating within a framework and under a supervisory regime. There is usually someone they should consult if in doubt; they are not just relying on their own initiative and judgement. As you will see in Unit 19, there are usually guidelines they should be following. It is their responsibility to know what the guidelines say and to follow them – and to know whom they should report to and to do so. Most care workers also have access to records about service users which they can use to find out about the person's situation and history, as you will see in Unit 18. These are ways in which organisations try to ensure that they offer good-quality care. In the next units you examine these practices in detail and consider whether they do actually contribute to making care safer.

Learning skills: Are you remembering enough?

Most students worry at times about whether they are remembering enough of the material they study. If you have concerns about your memory, then Activity 17 should be helpful. It gives you an opportunity to follow an online discussion about memory among previous students. Reading about other people's concerns is a good way of putting your own in perspective.

DVD

Activity 17   Is my memory good enough?

Allow about 20 minutes

This activity is presented in the form of a question-and-answer session on the topic of memory, with questions put by past students and replies from me (Andrew Northedge). (This activity is optional.)

Find Block 5, Unit 17, Activity 17 on the DVD.

Comment

Although at this point you may have only a hazy memory of units you studied just a few weeks ago, this is quite normal. Your mind is taken up with the challenges of each new unit, so things that you read earlier are bound to slide out of focus. As one student said, 'The more I read, the more I forget'. But this is inevitable – your mind has to 'make space' for new material. However, when you put serious effort into pulling the key ideas and information together, a lot of it will come back quite easily. Having once understood an issue, a case study, or a discussion, you can reassemble those thoughts in your mind relatively quickly by giving yourself a few reminders. Rather than worry about your memory at this point, the most important thing is to focus on trying to *understand* what you study and to *highlight*, or *underline* or *take notes*. By doing these things and by writing your essays, you will gradually lodge in your mind the ideas and themes of K101 along with related information. As you may remember from Section 4.2 of *The Good Study Guide*, learning is not about memorising, but about understanding and using ideas. (You might find it useful to look again at the key points boxes on pages 81–2; also at the key points box on pages 147–8.)

Reader

Learning skills: Memory in the exam

You will have seen that some students in Activity 17 linked their memory concerns to the exam. One of them wrote '... the exam is going to be different. I just know that I am going to forget everything.' However, as far as K101 is concerned, you don't need to worry about this. As you saw in Unit 12, when you looked at the information about the exam in the Assessment Guide, you are encouraged to take a sheet of notes into the exam with you. If you follow the guidance in Unit 23 on revising the course systematically and if you then make summary notes on the 'Examination notes sheet', you will have just the triggers you need in order to bring what you have learned back to mind.

End-of-unit checklist

Studying this unit should have helped you to:

- suggest ways in which intimate care can be provided sensitively and with regard to service users' dignity and preferences
- discuss why intimate care can be particularly problematic
- explain what is meant by 'challenging behaviour' and what implications it has for how carers should respond to it
- explain why some care settings can become systematically harmful to service users.

References

Action on Elder Abuse (2001) *You're Never Too Old to Hurt*, London, Action on Elder Abuse.

Barnett, A. (2006) 'Whistleblower accuses staff of "appalling" abuse at care home', *Observer*, 19 February [online], www.guardian.co.uk/society/2006/feb/19/longtermcare.uknews (Accessed 26 June 2008).

Bissell, L., Phillips, N. and Stenfert Kroese, B. (2005) 'The experience of a man with severe challenging behaviour following a resettlement from hospital: a single case design', *British Journal of Learning Disabilities*, vol. 33, no. 4, pp. 166–73.

Daily Mail (2007) 'Six care workers sacked for whistleblowing awarded £1m', *Daily Mail*, 14 August [online], www.dailymail.co.uk/news/article-475310/Six-care-workers-sacked-whistleblowing-awarded-1m.html (Accessed 26 June 2008).

Department of Health (DH) (2000) *No Secrets: Guidance on Developing and Implementing Multi-agency Policies and Procedures to Protect Vulnerable Adults from Abuse*, London, The Stationery Office.

Department of Health (DH) (2003a) *Care Homes for Adults (18–65): National Minimum Standards and the Care Homes Regulations*, London, The Stationery Office.

Department of Health (DH) (2003b) *Care Homes for Older People: National Minimum Standards and the Care Homes Regulations 2001*, London, The Stationery Office.

General Social Care Council (2002) *Code of Practice for Social Care Workers and Code of Practice for Employers of Social Care Workers*, London, General Social Care Council.

Glendinning, C., Rummery, K., Halliwell, S., Jacobs, S. and Tyrer, J. (2000) *Buying Independence: Using Direct Payments to Purchase Integrated Health and Social Services*, Bristol, The Policy Press.

Harris, J., Allen, D., Cornick, M., Jefferson, A. and Mills, R. (1996) *Physical Interventions: A Policy Framework*, Kidderminster, British Institute of Learning Disabilities.

Harris, J., Cornick, M., Jefferson, A., Mills, R. and Paley, S. (2008) *Physical Interventions: A Policy Framework*, Kidderminster, British Institute of Learning Disabilities.

Lawler, J. (1991) *Behind the Screen: Nursing Somology and the Problem of the Body*, Melbourne, Churchill Livingstone.

Leece, J. and Bornat, J. (eds) (2006) *Developments in Direct Payments*, Bristol, The Policy Press.

Lowe, K. and Felce, D. (1995) 'The definition of challenging behaviour in practice', *British Journal of Learning Disabilities*, vol. 23, no. 3, pp. 118–23.

Meyer, M., Donelly, M. and Weerakoon, P. (2007) '"They're taking the place of my hands": perspectives of people using personal care', *Disability and Society*, vol. 22, no. 6, pp. 595–608.

Public Concern at Work (undated) *Whistleblowing Legislation, PCaW* [online], www.pcaw.co.uk/law/law.htm (Accessed 26 June 2008).

Saxton, M., Curry, M.A., Powers, L.E., Maley, S., Eckels, K. and Gross, J. (2001) '"Bring my scooter so I can leave you" – a study of disabled women handling abuse by personal assistance providers', *Violence against Women*, vol. 7, no. 4, pp. 393–417.

Scourfield, P. (2005) 'Implementing the Community Care (Direct Payments) Act: will the supply of Personal Assistants meet the demand and at what price?', *Journal of Social Policy*, vol. 34, no. 3, pp. 469–88.

Skills for Care (2005) *HSC336 Contribute to the Prevention and Management of Abusive and Aggressive Behaviour*, National Occupational Standards Health and Social Care [online], www.skillsforcare.org.uk/files/HSC0336%20adult%20abusive%20aggressive%20behav.pdf (Accessed 5 August 2008).

Twigg, J. (2000) 'Carework as a form of bodywork', *Ageing and Society*, vol. 20, no. 4, pp. 389–411.

Twigg, J. (2006) *The Body in Health and Social Care*, Basingstoke, Palgrave Macmillan.

UNISON (2003) *Duty of Care: A Handbook to Assist Health Care Staff Carrying out their Duty of Care to Patients, Colleagues and Themselves*, London, UNISON.

Unit 18

Handling personal information

Prepared for the course team by Rebecca Jones

Contents

Introduction

This unit examines the role that records about service users play in making care safer. Records may seem quite boring and mundane, but I hope this unit will help you realise that they are actually interesting and important. They are also very personal – they are all about individuals. People can have very strong feelings about records, as you will see. In this unit you will be looking at questions such as:

- how it feels to have records kept about you

- who gets to write records

- who gets to see records

- whether computerised records make care safer and better

- what sort of information in personal records needs to be kept confidential

- how it feels to have your confidential information shared.

Keeping records has always been a major part of health and social care work but it has become even more important in recent years. Wider changes in society, such as an increased fear of litigation, less willingness to just trust care professionals to get on with their jobs, and demands for more accountability from care workers (a topic you will study in Unit 19), mean that there is more pressure on care workers to keep comprehensive records. There have also been changes in the law that give people more rights to see information stored about them.

In the first section of this unit you will consider why personal records are so important in health and social care. In the second section you will explore the experience of keeping records and having records kept about you. You will see that keeping good-quality records can have an important role in making care safer. The third section looks at the growth of electronically stored personal records and how this is different from traditional paper-based records. The final section examines how the information contained in personal records should be shared with other people and other organisations. It focuses particularly on confidentiality and whether service users have given their consent to information about them being shared.

Core questions

- Why do we need personal records in health and social care?

- Why is keeping good records a skilled and important part of care work?

- What difference does it make when personal records are kept electronically?

- In what circumstances should personal information about a service user be shared with other people?

Are you taking the IVR?

If you are studying K101 as part of the Integrated Vocational Route (IVR), don't forget to check your VQ Candidate Handbook to see which Unit 18 activities contribute to your electronic portfolio.

1 Why do we need records?

People often have strong feelings about the place of record keeping in health and social care. In this section you will look at some of these feelings and ask what role records can play in making care safer.

People often complain about the amount of paperwork they have to do in their jobs; health and social care workers are no exception. You may have heard care workers complain that they spend so much of their time filling in forms that they have no time to do the 'real' work that was the reason they wanted the job in the first place. You may have said this yourself.

Facing the paperwork mountain

Newspapers regularly carry articles claiming that care workers spend too much time on paperwork and not enough on working directly with service users.

Activity 1   What's the problem?

Allow about 15 minutes

Look at the extracts from newspaper articles. What do they say is the problem with paperwork? Make some notes to help you answer this question.

Comment

Although these articles are fairly short they make quite a lot of claims about the problems with paperwork. I noted the following:

- Health and social care workers spend too large a proportion of their time on paperwork and too little with service users.
- It's inefficient when records are handwritten.
- It seems that records are designed to avoid litigation, not to help service users.
- Care workers feel torn between their desire to work with people and the requirement to keep records.
- Spending too much time recording information can prevent workers from building a good relationship with service users.

Paperwork mountain keeps nurses from care

Jo Revill, health editor

Sunday 27 November 2005   The Observer
http://observer.guardian.co.uk/uk_news/stry/0,,1651769,00.html

Nurses are being overloaded with paperwork and administrative tasks, with as much as 40 per cent of their working week diverted from patient care.

A study looking at how nurses spend their days is expected to show many hours each week are wasted filing, answering the phone and preparing documents rather than on bedside care. Nurses are now expected to record every health 'event', and even a simple decision to admit a patient on to a ward can mean an hour of form filling.

As hospitals are not yet fully computerised, notes are still mostly handwritten. They then have to be filed - largely to protect the NHS from litigation if anything goes wrong.

The general secretary of the Royal College of Nursing, Dr Beverley Malone, warned this weekend that paperwork is taking too much time. She said hospitals needed to employ more clerks to take pressure off the nursing staff, so that they could get back to talking to patients and their relatives.

'The administrative burden is keeping them from doing the things that need to be done, whether it's tackling patient safety or infection control or talking to patients. It seems like it's taking up an incredible amount of their time. There are more clerical tasks, more documentation, and targets to meet – and targets are important, but they mean documentation.'

Malone has spoken to ministers and says they are keen to find a solution but that so far nothing has happened. It is mostly left to individual trusts to decide whether nurses are spending too much time on documentation.

Malone said: 'It's a double whammy for nurses. They want to provide the care for patients but get tied up in administrative responsibilities. But if you're there to hold someone's hand and talk to the patient about the surgery they are facing, we know that they are going to get better clinical results

Feeling overwhelmed by paperwork

'This back-covering paperwork with its inquisitorial style is actually dangerous'

Wednesday 27 November 2002
http://society.guardian.co.uk/publicvoices/childprotection/story/0,,848328,00.html

Hazel Lamb, 52, is a family social worker of 27 years' standing working in Sussex

… We are doing this extensive form-filling at a time when everyone involved is upset and in need of some immediate service. Only the most skilled social worker will be able to fill in all the necessary questionnaires without leaving the family feeling it has been bombarded with questions. Social workers need time and space to listen, observe and reflect on their observations, working with parents and liaising with other agencies to provide care geared to the situation. From where I sit in social services, it seems that as soon as a person is referred to us the government's main interest is to collect all sorts of information. So it bombards social workers with questions, we bombard clients with questions, and what is lost sight of is providing the actual service …

- The process of filling in a lot of forms can be distressing to service users.
- Records are not part of 'the actual service'.

You may have thought of other reasons as well from your own observations and experiences.

Clearly, record keeping can cause problems for care workers and care users. But people also seem to get very upset if good records are not kept.

National jabs scandal exposed
By Jane Simmons
8 November 2006
The Sun
CHILD immunisation records are in such chaos that health chiefs across Britain have no idea what jabs have been given to hundreds of thousands of kiddies. This scandal is exposed in top secret documents leaked to The Sun, which reveal records held by NHS officials are a farce.

Warning over medical record blunders
6 May 2004
The Daily Mail
Patients need to check their medical records to identify errors that could have serious implications for their future treatment, employment and insurance, campaigners have urged. *Which?* said they had evidence of mistakes made in records, including one man who found out he had apparently had a cervical smear test.

Patient's records falsified – inquest informed
15 May 2007
Milton Keynes Citizen
A staff member at a city psychiatric unit falsified observation records on an at-risk patient who killed himself, an inquest has been told.

You can see from these newspaper extracts that not keeping good records can make care very unsafe. So it seems it does matter that care records are kept and that those records are accurate. In the next activity you are going to explore why records are so important in health and social care settings.

Activity 2   Why are records important?

Allow about 25 minutes

In the first column of the grid below are some reasons why records are needed in health and social care. The second and third columns are blank for you to fill in. Think about the different health and social records that exist about you and your family or friends and, in each row of the second column, write down an example from your own experience. Then, in the third column, write what might happen in general if records were not kept. The first row is filled in for you as an example.

Why we need records	Example from my life	Problems that might arise if no records were kept
So that service users' histories are not forgotten and can be used to inform care	My GP's record of health problems I had as a child which still sometimes affect me	The best care might not be given. Dangerous or harmful care could be provided. Service users might feel that their experiences and stories were not being taken into account.
So that service users can check what has happened to them and what services they are supposed to be receiving		
So that care workers can remember what they have done in the past, what they have agreed to do in the future, and when things are happening		
So that care can be provided by more than one person		
So that care can be coordinated between different agencies		
Because signed records can prove that something has happened or been agreed		
To provide information which improves public health		

Comment

Here are some answers from our course testers.

Why we need records	Example from my life	Problems that might arise if no records were kept?
So that service users' histories are not forgotten and can be used to inform care	My GP's record of health problems I had as a child which still sometimes affect me	The best care might not be given. Dangerous or harmful care could be provided. Service users might feel that their experiences and stories were not being taken into account.
So that service users can check what has happened to them and what services they are supposed to be receiving	When my aunt came out of hospital she didn't seem to be getting all the care we had been told she would receive. I was able to look at her care plan and see that some agencies had not contacted her.	Service users might not be able to remember everything they need to know. If there were no written record, they might find it more difficult to complain if they were not getting services that had been agreed.

So that care workers can remember what they have done in the past, what they have agreed to do in the future, and when things are happening	My antenatal records which laid out when antenatal tests had happened and which ones were coming up	Details and even major issues might be forgotten. Time would be wasted finding out the same information again. Repeating some forms of care, such as medical treatments, unnecessarily could be harmful.
So that care can be provided by more than one person	When I was having a course of physiotherapy I usually saw the same person. But one time she was off sick and her colleague was able to see me instead.	Most people in health and social care settings work in teams, and without records this would be very difficult. Mistakes and unsafe kinds of care would be much more likely to occur if there were only verbal 'handovers'.
So that care can be coordinated between different agencies	When my aunt was readmitted to hospital someone informed her home carers and the Meals on Wheels service	Time and resources would be wasted. Essential services would not be provided. In cases of abuse, connections would not be made between concerns raised by people from different agencies.
Because signed records can prove that something has happened or been agreed	I signed a consent form before having my wisdom teeth removed	Without signed records, organisations would find it harder to protect themselves from being sued. Service users would find it harder to prove what has been agreed with them.
To provide information which improves public health	My health visitor has a record of my son's vaccinations	The information needed for public health promotion schemes would not be available.

So records in health and social care can serve many useful purposes and play an important part in making care safer. When people have lived in institutions for long periods of their lives, the official records created by that institution can provide one source of information that helps service users make sense of their experiences, as you saw in the cases of Lennox Castle and Jordan's life story book (Unit 5).

Most people would probably agree that health and social care organisations do need to keep records of some sort. But, as you saw at the beginning of this section, too much record keeping can be very time-consuming and can create other problems. The challenge is to work out what needs to be recorded and what doesn't, and how to keep those records in the most effective way. There are no easy answers to these questions because it depends on what the record is for and the situation in which it is to be used. In the next section you will continue to think about records by looking at how they work in practice.

Key points

- People often think of record keeping as distracting from 'real' care work.

- But people also want good records to be kept.

- Record keeping plays an important part in making care safer.

2 Experiencing records

What is it like to have records kept about you? Why is it so difficult to keep good records? Can you always see your own records? Who makes personal records? These are some of the questions explored in this section.

2.1 Records in action

To start, you will look at record keeping in everyday life. The next two activities are on the DVD.

DVD

Activity 3   The first visit

Allow about 20 minutes

You are going to see a health visitor, Christine Fuller, making her first visit to new parents Amy Bird and Brian Peters.

Find Block 5, Unit 18, Activity 3 on the DVD.

Comment

Quite a lot of different records are being created and referred to in this scene. You can already see that using records while interacting with service users can be challenging for care workers. You can also see that what is written on their official record can provoke strong emotions in service users.

Keeping records is an important part of most care worker's responsibilities. For many workers it is a contractual requirement that they keep good records. Since Christine is working within the NHS in England, she is obliged to follow the guidance issued by the Department of Health about managing records (DH, 2006). There is equivalent guidance for the other nations of the UK and for people working in social care. Care workers who are members of a registered profession, such as nurses, health visitors, social workers and occupational therapists, are also obliged to follow the guidance about record keeping which is issued by their professional body. So Christine also has to follow the guidance from the Nursing and Midwifery Council (2007). Care workers who are not members of a profession are often also required to keep records of some sort, even if recording only 'AWOL' ('all well on leaving') in a small box, as many home carers do.

Records are an important part of working in an interdisciplinary team; they enable workers with different skills and different responsibilities to work together with service users. The hospital discharge letter gave Christine some information to help her begin to form her own relationship with Amy and Brian: for a start it told her where they lived and that they had a 10-day-old baby. Sometimes records are created from scratch, but sometimes they build on existing records. Most records are created by workers rather than service users, but, as you will see in Section 2.3, this isn't always the case. Because record keeping can be so time-consuming, *records are always only a partial account of what is going on* – they don't cover everything that happens at a meeting. They usually prioritise the information that interests the worker and their organisation so that they can fulfil their role, rather than what the service user thinks is most important to record. As you have already seen with Amy, this can be unhelpful and even distressing to service users.

DVD

Activity 4   The same first visit?

Allow about 20 minutes

Now return to the DVD to see Christine, Amy and Brian's thoughts about the visit immediately afterwards.

Find Block 5, Unit 18, Activity 4 on the DVD.

Comment

The different people saw the visit quite differently. The record showed relatively little of what went on during the visit but what it did show was closer to Christine's perspective than to Amy or Brian's.

Making records tends to reduce a complex situation to something much more straightforward and manageable. But even when a record is supposed to keep account of something quite straightforward, it's not always easy to keep good records in practice (Garfinkel, 1967).

You may have noticed in the video scenes that Christine is filling in two records at once: the red book, which she leaves with Amy, and the white form, which she takes away with her. She doesn't make as many comments on the white form as

---

Amberside NHS
Primary Care Trust

CHILD HEALTH SUMMARY

DATA SET LABELS

NUM 458977 Male 3560 gms   1/10/07
BIRD *PETERS Zac*
53 BEECH LANE
KITFORD, AMBERSIDE
AB4 9QT
GP G99999 DR DUSTIN
HV 111   NHS NO 123 456 7890

FAMILY STRUCTURE (Parents/Carers/Siblings)

Brian 8/3/72

Ethnicity/Language

Mother
Father
Child

FAMILY MEDICAL HISTORY (Refer p6 PCHR)

Nil of note

DV discussed?   [Yes]   [No]   EPDS score (6-8 weeks)

Refer Family Card [Yes]   [No]

Signature   Date

FEEDING HISTORY

Breastfed	Birth	PBV	6-8/52	3/12	6/12	Date of solids
Fully	✓	✓				
Partially						
Bottle only						

BIRTH DETAILS

Baby Bird *Peters*
H12345678
Amberside Hospital
BW 3560   DOB 1/10/07
MOTHER'S DOB 30/9/75
Gest. age 39 + 5

NEONATAL

TYPE OF DELIVERY *Normal* APGAR 9 + 9

SCBU   No. of days
          Reason:

VIT K   ORAL (IM)   (BIRTH)
          7 DAYS   4 WEEKS

NEONATAL SCREENING

		DATE
PKU	Neg / Pos	8/10/07
TSH	Neg / Pos	8/10/07
CF	Neg / Pos	8/10/07
HAEMOGLOBINOPATHY	Neg / Pos	8/10/07
HEARING SCREEN	*Pass*	2/10/07

8 MONTH HEARING TEST   Date:

Result: HV Service / Audiology (please circle)

Signature (if by HV Service)

IMMUNISATIONS

BCG
DTP/Hib/MENC/POLIO
DTP/Hib/MENC/POLIO
DTP/Hib/MENC/POLIO
MMR   PSB
OTHER

PRIMARY VISIT   Date: *11/10/0*
Expedictomy fore

Signature: *Christin John*

6-8 WEEK REVIEW   Date:

Weight: Centile:

HC   Centile:

Signature:

GP Result:

1 YEAR REVIEW   Date:

Weight: Centile:

Signature:

2 YEAR REVIEW

Child seen/not seen   Date:

Signature:

CONGENITAL/MEDICAL CONDITIONS

The 'white form' as it looked by the end of the day

in the red book, even though she explains that it is her record of what's in the red book. In fact, she made more additions to the white form once she got back to her office after making another call. In the next activity you are going to look at this filled-in version of the white form that existed by the end of the day.

Activity 5   The form
Allow about 10 minutes

Look at the record that Christine created. What do you notice about how it has been filled in and how it relates to the scene you saw? Are there any sections that don't seem to have been filled in correctly? Why do you think this might have happened?

Comment

I was particularly struck by the way in which all the different things that people said got reduced to a few tick boxes, words and abbreviations on the form. The emotion that Amy felt didn't appear at all and neither did her account of the difficult birth experience. But, as you have already seen, records have to be as brief as possible while still containing all the necessary information. Otherwise they would take too long to make and to read.

There are some mistakes on the form. It states that Zac is fully breastfed but Amy said that they give him bottles sometimes. It also has Zac's surname wrong, as Brian pointed out. Mistakes like this are very common on records and sometimes even apparently minor mistakes about names or dates of birth can have enormous consequences, as you will see in the case study in the next section. Mistakes are particularly common when records are wholly or partly filled in afterwards, as in this case. Of course, there can be very good reasons why workers fill in records after they have seen service users, rather than at the time. It's hard to pay someone full attention while also filling in a form, and service users may find someone apparently concentrating on a form intimidating and off-putting.

You may also have noticed that some sections of the form weren't filled in at all. You have already heard Christine explain why she didn't ask the question on her form about domestic violence. You may think that Christine should have asked this question. Perhaps she could have created an opportunity to talk to Amy on her own. Presumably the question is on the form because the NHS Trust she works for has decided that this is important information that should be asked routinely and needs to be stored. Screening for domestic violence like this is a good way of identifying people who are being abused (Price et al., 2007) and this is part of making sure service users are safe. While Christine may intend to explore this issue at a later meeting, as she claims, there might be all sorts of reasons why that never happens. However, you heard her say that she finds asking about domestic violence on a first visit is too abrupt and that Brian's presence throughout the visit made it difficult.

Care workers from different professional groups often have different traditions about how to fill in forms. For example, social workers have traditionally written more discursive and descriptive notes than nurses, who traditionally use a lot of abbreviations and devices such as colour codes. (If you are interested in colour codes, see Davey, 2000, for an example.) In addition, groups of care workers often develop their own unofficial ideas about 'how to fill in these forms' and new members of the team quickly pick up these ideas and continue them. For example, someone who used to work in a care home for older people told me that there was a section on their form headed 'sexualisation'. She commented that workers always seemed to write 'no problems' or 'not interested' for men and 'likes to look nice' for women. If you work in a care setting, you might like to spend a few minutes thinking about what the norms are for the way you fill in your forms and whether these norms are actually helpful.

Care workers have to use their judgement to decide how to deliver the best service overall and what weight to place on different parts of the written record. If you have worked in care you might be able to think of occasions when you didn't fill a form in properly and knew that you had a good reason for your action. Using forms in real life often involves making sensitive adjustments between an ideal situation and what is actually feasible or sensible.

To sum up, people often dismiss record making as a routine or boring part of care work – they imply that it is not 'real' or skilled care work. But actually, making records in real-life situations can be very challenging and requires good professional judgement about what really matters (Berg, 1996).

2.2 Getting hold of your own record

Record-keeping systems are usually designed to foster the efficient working of staff and the organisations in which they work. They are the legal property of whoever creates them. However, they are also very important to service users – after all, most records are about service users in one way or another. In the past, it was quite rare for service users to know what was in their health and social care records. But in recent years there has been a growing recognition that service users have a right to see their own records (except in a few specific circumstances, as you will see later in this section). Studies have found that having access to their records helps service users better understand their care and improves communication with care workers (Essex et al., 1990; Grange et al., 1998; Ross and Lin, 2003). Some people argue that one of the best ways of making care genuinely user-centred is to ensure service users have access to their own records (Berg, 2002). There have also been changes to the law that strengthen service users' rights to see their own records and records about an organisation. You can find out more about this by looking at the information on the Data Protection Act 1998 and the Freedom of Information Act 2000 in the HSC Resource Bank or by looking them up on the internet.

If service users do see their own records, they can correct the sort of mistakes described in the example below.

'Half my records weren't about me – they were a shambles!'

'I'd gone to the doctor about a minor matter and he asked if I'd ever been in hospital. I said only for an operation for an abscess at the base of the spine. He looked in the notes and said "I was thinking of the other hospital". I said what hospital? He said: "It says here you were an inpatient in a mental hospital for 6 months." I told him I'd never been in a mental hospital. I got the impression he didn't believe me.

'I asked him if he had the details of my operation in the notes. There was nothing. Then he examined me, saw the operation scar, and that made him believe there might be something wrong with the records. The problem I'd been operated on for flared up again 4 or 5 years later, and that wasn't there either. He went through parts of it that were all wrong. I said "I've never had a doctor in that area. That was never *my* doctor. None of that applies to me." It wasn't just the odd sheet. I discovered that about half of my records weren't about me. There was obviously a shambles.'

'The GP got in touch with the medical records section. He discovered that parts of the record referred to another person of the same name with a similar birthdate. We both appear to have been with the same doctor at one time.

'Could I have been given the wrong treatment at any time as a result of the incorrect information contained in "my" notes? Could some treatment have been withheld for the same reason?

'I have always been in the habit of agreeing to prospective employers writing to my doctor concerning my health. Did the answers they received ever unjustly prejudice them concerning me? If you've applied for a serious job and they see you've been in treatment for mental problems it could cause all kinds of problems.'

(Campaign for Freedom of Information, 1990)

While such major mistakes are probably quite rare, they are much more likely to be spotted and corrected if service users have easy access to their own records. So how do you go about getting access to your records? As you will see in Section 2.3, some records are held by service users anyway, and consequently are always accessible to them. But most are still held by agencies such as GP surgeries, hospitals and clinics, and are not usually seen by service users. You are now going to look at some of the issues to do with service users accessing their own records. Dan Morgan is someone you will meet again in more detail in Unit 20.

Introducing Dan Morgan

Dan Morgan is 28 and White British. He is a heavy user of amphetamine sulphate ('speed'), which causes him to behave in ways that other people find bizarre. He gets some support from the local authority drug problem team and a local voluntary organisation. He is currently unemployed but sometimes finds casual work. He has no fixed address and often sleeps rough, although at the moment he is staying with his mother. He is registered with the same GP as his mother. Recently, his mother secretly made an appointment to see their GP to discuss Dan's increasingly erratic behaviour. She was so worried about him that she couldn't sleep and was having panic attacks. The GP made some entries on his mother's record and he also made an entry on Dan's record about some of the details she told him. A few weeks later, Dan decides that he wants to know what it says in his GP records about his drug use.

If his GP agrees, Dan could of course just look over his shoulder at the computer screen during a consultation. But if Dan wants to study his records at leisure and have his own copy, or if his GP is unwilling to show him informally, he would have to make a formal application under the provisions of the Data Protection Act 1998. This could be in person or in writing and he might have to provide proof of his identity. He might also have to pay a fee if there had been no additions to the record in the previous 40 days. The amount varies depending on how the records are held and in 2007 would have been between £10 and £50 (DH, 2003c). Although the legislation involved is different in the different nations of the UK, the implications for service users are very similar. A sum of £10 to £50 is not huge, but it might be a significant hurdle for Dan, who doesn't have much spare money, and to other service users with very limited incomes.

Even if Dan did manage to get the money from somewhere, there are still some reasons why he might not see all of his health record. Here is some of the relevant guidance from the Department of Health:

> Q   Are there any circumstances in which information contained in health records may be withheld from the data subject?

> A   Under the Data Protection Act 1998 there are certain circumstances in which the record holder may withhold information. Access may be denied, or limited, where the data controller[*] judges that information in the records would cause serious harm to the physical or mental health or condition of the patient, or any other person, or where giving access would disclose information relating to or provided by a third person who had not consented to the disclosure. Data controllers must be prepared to justify decisions to withhold information.

> Q   Where information has been withheld are record holders obliged to advise applicants that this is the case?

> A   No. Record holders are free to advise applicants of the grounds on which information has been withheld but are not obliged to do so. If it is thought likely to cause undue distress the record holder may not wish to volunteer the fact that information has been withheld.

> (DH, 2008)

*A data controller is the person who is registered as responsible for the data; in Dan's GP practice this is the practice manager.

So Dan's GP doesn't have to release any information that he can argue would cause Dan or someone else serious harm. When Dan's mother saw the GP to talk about her worries she did not want Dan to know about it, in case he reacted violently to her getting involved. So there are two reasons why the part of Dan's record that refers to his mother's visit could be withheld from him: the GP could possibly argue that Dan's mother would be at risk of serious harm; and he could certainly argue that she has not given consent to the information she provided being disclosed. Dan would not necessarily know that part of his record was missing though. The second question and answer in the quote from the Department of Health above says that the record holder does not have to tell the service user if some information has been withheld.

The records Dan wants to see are health records. If he wanted to see his social services record, very similar rules would apply. You might remember from Unit 5 that Jordan Morgan's social worker, Suzanne McGladdery, says that maybe Jordan shouldn't see all the parts of his record until he is a little older because he would find it very distressing.

Although service users have the right to see most parts of their health and social care records, it is still relatively uncommon for this to happen. Even if they do manage to see them, the records may be kept in ways that make them difficult to understand. Jargon and abbreviations make it quicker for care workers to fill in forms and this can mean that they have more time to spend relating directly to service users. But it can also make it impossible for service users to understand what is being said about them in their records. Service users who do not speak English or whose English is limited – like Mina Ali whom you met in Unit 10 – will probably have difficulty understanding their care records, especially if they contain a lot of jargon and abbreviations. In addition, some people need information in a particular format such as Braille, large fonts, on tape or in language and pictures that make it easier for someone with learning disabilities to use. The provisions of the Disability Discrimination Act 1995 mean that service providers have to make reasonable adjustments to ensure that any information they provide is accessible to disabled people. But a study on the NHS carried out in 2002 found that very little health information was accessible, including patients' own records (Clark, 2002).

Increasingly, some records are held by service users. As you saw in the video scenes for Activities 3 and 4, the 'red book', which is one of the main records of Zac's health, is kept by his mother, Amy. Records about antenatal care, home dialysis and diabetes care are commonly held by service users themselves. In social care, the record of home carers' visits and the tasks they undertake on a particular visit is usually left with the service user.

2.3 Making your own record

When service users hold their own records, they sometimes also make their own additions to those records. For example if Amy's baby, Zac, later developed a problem with bed-wetting, Amy might be asked to keep a record as part of a programme designed to help with this. Zac might even make his own contribution to the record by sticking stars onto a chart that recorded his continence. Some people with diabetes test and record their own blood sugar levels and manage their own medication, as Anwar Malik, whom you met in Unit 2, did for a while. People who experience depression or panic attacks are sometimes asked to keep diaries about how they are feeling, like the one shown in Figure 1.

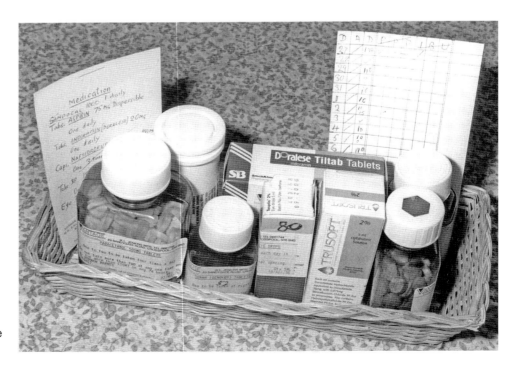

This person created his own record of which medications to take when, in order to manage his own care

People sometimes create their own informal record, especially if their care is complicated; for example having to remember to take lots of different medicines at different times. Bill Bytheway et al. (2000) did some research into how older people managed their medication and they took the photograph below, which shows how one person created his own record.

Similarly, people with learning disabilities may create and keep 'hospital books' – their own accessible records that they can take with them into hospital.

Diary sheet

Please make an entry whenever you notice a definite increase in anxiety

Date/time	Description of situation	Anxiety level: 0–10	Description of (a) physical feelings (b) thoughts	Coping method	Anxiety level after: 0–10

Figure 1   A diary to record anxiety levels that service users fill in themselves

Sometimes service users are the best people to make records about themselves. For instance, records concerned with how someone is feeling are clearly best made by that person.

While most users of services might be expected to be honest and accurate in making their own records, there are some situations where this is not always the case. For example, people with kidney failure have to keep a record of how much they eat and drink between dialysis sessions because this affects their treatment; but these records may not always be very accurate. This may partly be because it is time-consuming and boring to have to record everything you eat and drink, week in week out. But it may also be because patients suspect that people who stick to their diet and fluid regimes are more likely to be selected for transplants or home dialysis. This provides a very strong incentive to lie, or to 'forget' some snacks or a few drinks. Clinic staff have to assess a patient's condition by using other sources of information as well as food diaries – for example weight, blood tests and physical examinations. Including these additional checks means that the risk of patients falsifying their record sheets is reduced, or at least falsifications are more likely to be spotted.

In certain situations it can simply be too unsafe for people to make their own records. Some people who are addicted to heroin are prescribed methadone and other drugs to help them to manage their addiction. When a GP prescribes methadone, they are likely to ask the patient about their recent use of heroin, but it would not be safe to rely on this information alone. The GP will probably also require independent evidence from a urine test. Some people are too ill or too confused to make their own records and not all people receiving services want to be involved in record keeping, even if they are given support in doing so.

So far in this unit you have looked at why records are necessary, what it's like to keep records and to have records kept about you, and some of the issues about service users making their own records. In the next section you will continue to think about these themes by looking at a particular form of record keeping – on computers and via the internet.

Key points

- Creating and maintaining records is an integral and skilled part of care work.

- Records are always only a partial account of a complex reality and are designed to do a particular job, not to fully represent every relevant circumstance.

- Service users have the right to access their own records, except in some particular circumstances.

- It can be empowering and useful for service users to add to their own records, or to create them themselves.

3 Electronic records

The growth in access to computers and the internet has led to changes in how a lot of personal care records are held. This section looks at the move towards electronic records and the significance this can have for service users and care workers.

3.1 Keeping records electronically

It is increasingly common for service user records to be held electronically.

DVD

Activity 6 Exploring an electronic service user record

Allow about 40 minutes

In this activity you will examine an electronic record about the care of people with renal (kidney) problems.

Find Block 5, Unit 18, Activity 6 on the DVD.

Comment

You saw that this electronic record contains a lot more information than a paper one usually does. Provided that the people using it have internet access, it is much more accessible than a paper record.

Renal Patient View gives patients the same access to their record as their GP and clinic staff have. But not all electronic service user records are instantly accessible by service users in this way. Some are more like a paperless version of ordinary records. They are usually seen only by workers although, as you read in Section 2, service users may ask to see their records.

Electronic records have the potential to be more accessible to service users than paper records, where there is just one set of papers in a folder and this folder has to be moved to the right place. Electronic records can be accessed from any place

Some electronic records are very similar to traditional paper-based records. Service users don't usually have good access to them.

that has the right computer access, as long as the person looking is authorised to see them.

Reader

Activity 7   Advantages and disadvantages of electronic records
Allow about 40 minutes

Read Chapter 22 'Patients' experiences of accessing their electronic records', by Cecilia Pyper, Justin Amery, Marion Watson and Claire Crook in the Reader (pages 181–90). Drawing on the chapter and your own opinions, make two lists:

(a) the advantages of electronic service user records

(b) their disadvantages.

Then add your observations from Renal Patient View to the lists of advantages and disadvantages.

Comment

There are many possible advantages and disadvantages. The lists below are my ideas, but your list might look quite different.

(a) Advantages

- **Better access.** Renal Patient View allows everyone involved to access the records whenever they need to and wherever they are (as long as they have internet access and are able to use a computer). Although patients in the Reader chapter mainly viewed their records at the doctors' surgery, and therefore didn't have the freedom to access their records whenever they wanted, they still felt that better access was one of the benefits of electronic records. For visually impaired people, electronic records might be more accessible than traditional paper records if they have the right computer software to read them.

- **Legibility.** These records are all typed, so there are no problems with reading people's handwriting.

- **Possibly better outcomes.** The patients described in the Reader chapter felt that seeing their electronic health record could improve their relationship with their GP. They also thought it would improve the accuracy of records and help patients to manage their own care better. Of course, this could also be the case if they saw their own paper-based record but, as mentioned at the beginning of this section, seeing your own record can be easier to manage with electronic records. Electronic records can provide immediate access to test results. This might benefit people using Renal Patient View because seeing all their test results immediately might help someone to realise how their diet is affecting their test results. The same is true of other medical conditions, such as diabetes.

- **Collating information.** Storing information electronically should make it easier for organisations to audit and assess their performance. This may help to improve the *accountability* of services (a concept you will look at in detail in Unit 19).

- **Physical storage.** Electronic records take up much less physical storage space than paper-based records. Also, if they are properly backed up, there is always more than one copy of an electronic record, so records cannot be lost in the way that paper records can.

(b) Disadvantages

- **Dependence on internet access.** Better access for service users does depend on their having access to the internet. This might mean that less well-off and less computer-literate service users don't get the benefits. And this might increase inequalities in access to health and social care services. In particular, it might make access for some disabled people more difficult.

- **Information overload.** Records contain a lot of information, some of it very technical. Some people might find this overwhelming and it might make them more anxious about their condition or the services they receive. Records also usually contain abbreviations and specialist language, which service users might misunderstand (as in the examples in the Reader chapter).

- **Costs.** Although neither of the systems you have looked at cost anything for patients directly, there are significant costs to the NHS. Both hardware and software can be expensive and this is especially true for large centralised IT systems. The system needs maintenance and back-up, and staff need training in using it. There is also a cost in staff time showing service users how to use the system at the beginning. Digitising records which were originally paper-based is also costly.

- **Reliability.** Most electronic systems break down occasionally and that can have very serious consequences.

- **Security and confidentiality.** Although the authors of the Renal Patient View website try to be reassuring on the 'Help' page, nearly all computer systems can be hacked into by someone determined and knowledgeable enough. This was also a worry to the patients in the Reader chapter. The ease of access that is one of the major benefits of electronic records is also a possible disadvantage in that it may make records less secure. But of course paper records aren't necessarily very secure either.

So there are disadvantages to keeping records electronically as well as advantages. Electronic records are, however, increasingly common and are likely to become even more common in the future.

3.2 Integrated electronic records

Many agencies have made some use of electronic records for some years. These typically contain details such as a service user's name, address, date of birth, the services they are using and any named workers involved with them, such as a care manager or social worker. However, in recent years there has been a government-led push towards a more comprehensive type of electronic record – an integrated electronic service user record – as shown in Figure 2. These types of record are often known as electronic health records and electronic social care records.

Integrated electronic service user records are designed to gather together all the records about an individual that would previously have been kept by different agencies and in different locations. They include items such as case notes, records of visits made, care plans, results of tests, and enquiries and letters that are relevant to the person's care. The idea is that keeping all these different sources of information together and in electronic form will improve information sharing and accessibility. Clark (2002) points out that integrated electronic records could

Letters

Emails

Visit schedules

Mrs Jones needs a visit

Social worker case notes

Contact sheets

Audiovisual records

Computer records

Figure 2   An electronic social care record contains many more different types of record than a traditional paper record (DH, 2003b)

carry significant benefits for service users if they contain information about that person's preferences for the format in which they receive information. Visually impaired people who prefer information in Braille could automatically be sent their information in that format, whereas those who prefer their information in an audio format could receive tapes or CDs. These benefits could extend beyond disabled people to people who need information in languages other than English or people who have difficulty reading.

However, it is very difficult to develop a computer system that will allow information sharing to this extent without compromising service user confidentiality and security. Designing secure computer systems always involves trade-offs between security, cost and ease of use, so in practice no system is completely secure (Schneier, 2000). Even if a system is designed to be reasonably secure, people often share passwords, leave screens open and visible, or make simple mistakes which give them access to records they did not intend to look at (Foley, 2006).

Of course, traditional paper-based records are not necessarily stored very securely, but the difference with electronic records is that they can contain larger amounts of personal information in one place. The more comprehensive the records are, the more serious lapses of confidentiality can become. Many service users are concerned about the security and confidentiality of electronic records (Pyper et al., 2004).

Work on health care records is more advanced than on social care records, but even in health care there have been serious delays in creating integrated electronic records. For example, in 2003 it was hoped that every NHS patient in England would have an electronic patient record through the NHS Care Records Service by 2010 (NHS National Programme for Information Technology, 2003), but at the time of writing (2008) this is looking very unlikely. Nevertheless, even though there have been significant difficulties in making integrated electronic service user records work, they are likely to become more common and more important in the future.

Moment's blunder puts half the country at risk

21 November 2007
The Times

A junior official who appears to have been asleep on the job burnt the child benefit database onto two disks – and posted them …

Lost in the post – 25 million at risk after data discs go missing

21 November 2007
The Guardian
The government was forced to admit the most fundamental breach of faith between the state and citizen yesterday when it disclosed that the personal records of 25 million individuals, including their dates of birth, addresses, bank accounts and national insurance numbers had been lost in the post, opening up the threat of mass identity fraud and theft from personal bank accounts.

Now they've managed to lose the health records of hundreds of thousands of NHS patients

By DANIEL MARTIN
24 December 2007
The Daily Mail
The confidential records of hundreds of thousands of NHS patients and staff have gone missing in the latest data loss scandal to hit the Government.
Nine trusts admitted they have lost computer discs and memory sticks containing sensitive information during a Government-wide security review.
It comes only weeks after a series of high-profile data security incidents, including the loss of details of 25 million child benefit claimants.
The Department of Health said there was no proof that any of the data had fallen into the wrong hands.
But campaigners said the security breaches mean the Government should scrap plans for a centralised computer network containing all NHS records.

Electronic records can contain huge amounts of data compared with paper ones. This can mean that security lapses have much bigger effects.

Key points

- Keeping records electronically can make them much more accessible to both care workers and service users, as long as internet access is available.

- But there are also disadvantages to keeping records electronically, such as reliability and the more serious consequences of security breaches.

- Electronic service user records have the potential to contain additional types of information to traditional paper-based records.

Learning skills: Maintaining your K101 filing system

With all this talk about records and their uses, what about your own records? What do you actually do with your written records of your studies – your notes and TMAs, both on computer and on paper? Can you find your way to what you need, or has your past course work become a huge unsorted folder on your computer, plus a big pile of paper? Every student eventually needs an effective filing system. In many ways your filing system is more important than your memory. Nobody remembers everything, but clever students can find their way to *what* they need to know *when* they need to know it.

However, filing systems require some thought. A complicated system can be self-defeating – too time-consuming to maintain and too hard to recall when you need to find something. For both computer files and papers you need folder systems that are reasonably simple but also flexible, so that you aren't left with lots of items that don't fit anywhere. When you first start studying in a new area, you can't know what filing system is going to work well. Generally, it's best to start with a very straightforward system and then modify it as you go along. But have you been modifying your K101 filing system as the course has developed? Have you done any reorganising in recent weeks? Perhaps when you have finished this unit you should put aside a bit of time to tidy up. It will certainly be helpful, as you approach the exam, to have your files in reasonable order.

Computer files

If some of your K101 folders are getting so full that it's hard to find what you're looking for, it's easy to make a few new folders inside an overfull one, give them names, and then drag documents into them to tidy them away. Perhaps some of your older folders now don't seem to have quite the right names, because you have put things in them that you hadn't anticipated. If so, just rename them. An electronic filing system is immensely flexible. You can keep changing it around as you go along, as it becomes clear what is useful for your current needs. For example, when you have finished K101 you might create a 'Past courses' folder and drag your entire K101 folder into it. (If you can't remember how to make folders, or rename them, look it up in 'Getting started'.)

Paper files

Is it time to do some sorting of your papers and relabelling of your folders? With a supply of folders, sticky labels and boxes you can quite quickly create order out of a mound of course papers. Time you invest in this will quickly be repaid when you start trying to find things for revision purposes. Papers you can't find are barely worth having, but those you can locate quickly are often invaluable.

Organising files is more than a matter of ensuring quick access to information. It's a way of making yourself think about how a course is organised. By the time you have worked out an effective filing system, you have taught yourself something fairly fundamental about the nature and content of the course.

4 Sharing information from personal records

As you have seen, sharing information between different people and different services is one of the reasons we need records. But doing so raises questions about who gets to see different types of information and how service users can give consent to information from their personal records being shared. In this final main section of the unit you are going to look at some of the issues to do with sharing personal information.

Information sharing is crucial in health and social care work. For example, an important piece of guidance for people who work with children says:

> Sharing information is vital for early intervention to ensure that children and young people get the services they require. It is also essential to protect children and young people from suffering harm from abuse or neglect, and to prevent them from offending.

> (Department for Children, Schools and Families, 2007)

Service users also want their information to be shared appropriately. One course tester told the following story about his own experience.

Losing my voice

Having returned from a long holiday in India, following a week of illness I was admitted to my local hospital (in Scotland) with the suspicion that I had malaria. On my first day I lost my voice which meant I could only communicate by writing or whispering loudly and hoarsely. My wife and children were still in India and I was unable to speak to them before I was admitted, although I had let my brother know (he lives in London). I knew my wife was worried and so I initially had some friends phone her. However, after two days it was clear I was not going to be discharged for a while and so I spoke to staff about giving consent for them to let my wife know over the phone how I was doing. They said they couldn't do that and so I then wrote 'that I was giving informed consent for hospital staff to provide any medical information to my wife and brother when they rang'. I was then informed that they couldn't do that because it was against hospital policy.

I was slightly irate to put it mildly. I was of sound mind (although not body), I was providing explicit consent and so could not understand this refusal especially as it added to the stress of my wife and other family and thereby to mine. This to my view was not about a sound confidentiality policy, based on the rights and needs of clients, but one that had been written and adhered to irrespective of patients' rights.

As this story suggests, care workers sometimes find it hard to get the right balance between protecting someone's confidentiality and appropriately sharing information from their personal records. In the following section you will look at some of the principles which help care workers to make such judgements in everyday life.

Case workers sometimes find it hard to balance protecting confidentiality and appropriately sharing information

4.1 What is confidential information?

To begin with, consider what is meant by the term 'confidential information'. In everyday life we often use 'confidential' to mean 'secret' or 'not to be told to anyone'. But what about in health and social care settings? Here is one definition:

> Confidential information is information of some sensitivity, which is not already lawfully in the public domain or readily available from another public source, and which has been shared in a relationship where the person giving the information understood that it would not be shared with others.

(Department for Education and Skills, 2006, p. 9)

So, according to this definition, information is confidential if:

- it is sensitive
- it is not already publicly known
- the person gave the information in a setting where they expected confidentiality to be maintained.

You will explore further what this means in the following activities.

Activity 8   Is this information confidential?

Allow about 15 minutes

Read each of the situations below and try to work out whether, according to the definition above, the information is confidential.

(a) Two friends are meeting socially and one tells the other that a mutual friend's teenage daughter is pregnant.

(b) A home carer who works with older people is rung up by a friend for advice about her father who is finding it increasingly difficult to manage at home.

(c) A woman tells a nurse at a 'Well Woman' check-up that she has lost interest in sex recently.

(d) There has been a report in the local paper that a child's father has been found guilty of minor theft. The child tells a youth worker that their father has been caught stealing, saying, 'it's a secret – don't tell anyone'.

Comment

Definitions can be a helpful start to thinking about an issue and this is quite a good one, but all definitions can be hard to apply to real-life situations.

(a) I thought this situation probably wasn't confidential because the meeting is between two private individuals and there's no mention that this information shouldn't be passed on – it's gossip really.

(b) This is a bit trickier. On the one hand, this is an informal conversation between friends and the person asking for advice doesn't mention the information being confidential. But, on the other hand, the home carer is being asked because she has this job role and that might mean that the last bit of the definition applies: 'shared in a relationship where the person giving the information understood that it would not be shared with others'.

(c) This is much clearer. Most people treat information about sex as a sensitive topic and the situation is one where you would expect this sort of information not to be shared.

(d) This information is not confidential according to the definition because it is already in the public domain. But I thought that morally the youth worker might want to treat the information as confidential since the child has asked them to do so.

Although the definition is a useful starting point, once you try to apply it to real-life situations it can become more complicated. It makes a difference who the people are and whether someone acquires the information in their private life or in a job-related role. The definition is designed for use in work settings but dilemmas like this come up in private life as well. Some people might see confidentiality as an overarching moral principle that they apply at all times. For example, one course tester commented: 'I probably take it a bit far, but I tend to assume that everything remotely sensitive is confidential, even if someone has told it to me down the pub. I think I had confidentiality drummed into me so hard when I was training to be a Samaritan [telephone helpline volunteer for people who are desperate and suicidal] that it became part of who I am at all times.' In a work setting, though, employees and volunteers have responsibilities to pass on information as well as to keep the right information confidential. In Section 4.4 you will explore the question of passing on information when the person concerned has not given consent.

Another aspect of the definition that needs a bit more exploration is the phrase 'information of some sensitivity'. What sort of information is sensitive information? Is there a list somewhere of what this covers? You can get some ideas by looking at the definition of sensitive data used in the Data Protection Acts, which you can see in the HSC Resource Bank. For example, in the Data Protection Act 1998 as it applies in Scotland, sensitive data is defined as anything that is about people's:

- racial or ethnic origin
- political opinions
- religious beliefs or other beliefs of a similar nature
- trade union membership
- physical or mental health or condition
- sexual life
- offences or crimes.

However, this is a legal definition and what people actually feel is sensitive information about them can be different. The following activity will help you think through how you might assess what personal information counts as sensitive.

Activity 9   What are your sensitivities?

Allow about 10 minutes

Write down one or two pieces of information about yourself that you might want to be kept confidential – things that you wouldn't generally reveal about yourself. Then write down one or two pieces of information about yourself that you don't usually mind being generally known, but some people might be sensitive about.

Comment

Here are some of the answers our course testers gave.

Things I might want kept confidential:

- Twenty years ago I had major depression and was a voluntary patient in a mental hospital.
- My parents are German (I don't generally let people know this because I get so sick of the stupid comments about Heil Hitler, etc.).
- I've been trying to get pregnant for three years now.
- My brother committed suicide when I was 16.
- I'm a headmaster's daughter.
- My daughter's just told me she's a lesbian.
- My father was an alcoholic when I was growing up.

Things I don't usually mind if other people know:

- I'm diabetic.
- I've had serious depression in the past and tried to commit suicide.
- I'm bisexual.
- I'm an alcoholic, although I no longer drink.
- My daughter was conceived through IVF.
- I was a teenage mum.
- I've used drugs in the past, although I don't any more.

Clearly, different people find different types of personal information sensitive. While many people find some topics such as sexuality, suicide or family problems sensitive and are likely to want that information kept confidential, some people do not. You may have been surprised by some of the things people regard as sensitive information. I was certainly surprised by the comment about having German parents as this had never occurred to me before.

Of course, in doing this activity you have created your own record of personal information that you want to keep confidential. You might like to spend a few minutes reflecting on what you have just done. How did it feel to write these private things down? How would it have felt if someone else had written them down and taken the piece of paper away with them? What are you going to do with the piece of paper now?

Because different people regard different sorts of personal information as sensitive, you can't assume that you already know what information someone would want to be kept confidential. This leads to an important principle in dealing with confidential information: care workers need to ask service users how they want their personal information handled. This is essential if confidential information is going to be passed on to people who need to know but not to people who don't need to know.

4.2 Consent to sharing confidential information

Consent to sharing confidential information sounds like a fairly straightforward principle – people should be asked whether and in what circumstances they want information about themselves passed on. But it's a little more complicated once you apply it to the whole variety of health and social care settings.

Explicit consent

The most straightforward situation in which confidential information can be shared is when the people concerned have given their explicit consent for this to happen. Explicit consent means that the person gives consent knowing exactly what they are agreeing to. The person therefore needs to understand the implications of their information being shared, and this means that it has to be explained in terms that are relevant to service users, answering the questions that they need answered. In Unit 6 you saw an example of how explicit consent was negotiated in Chapter 23 in the Reader, 'Positive action', by Vijay K.P. Patel, which described the support group for boys who knew someone who was HIV-positive. The author talks about how important it was to make sure that the children and their families understood what was involved before they joined the group, because it would involve the boys knowing about and talking about their family member's illness. Here is an extract:

> … any child referred needed to be aware that there was someone in their family who was HIV positive. However before getting access to the children, the parent's trust and support needed to be gained … The quality of relationships that workers had with parents/carers was important in ensuring that the children understood that the important person/people in their lives trusted the workers and actively gave permission for the children to come knowing that HIV/AIDS would be mentioned and talked about … This whole process required a lot of time and even more flexibility. Fears around children being able to cope, children asking 'awkward questions' or telling everybody all had to be resolved.

(Reader, Chapter 23, p. 194)

In order to get explicit consent from the boys and their families to the boys taking part in the group, the workers had to put in a lot of time explaining what was involved. As they point out, it was important that the boys felt confident that their family members were also happy that they were sharing information about their HIV status. By spending a lot of time and effort, the workers could be reasonably confident that the boys and their families really were consenting to their personal information being shared.

Mental capacity and consent

In law, everyone is assumed initially to have the *capacity* to consent to things that affect them. Each time someone's consent is needed, the organisation involved has to make an assessment of whether the person is capable of making that particular decision on this particular occasion (and with the help of any support they need). You can't assume that people who have learning disabilities, young children or people who have dementia, for example, are incapable of consenting to something. You can find out more about the definitions and legislation concerned with mental capacity by searching in the HSC Resource Bank.

One way of trying to make sure that service users have understood that information about them will be shared is by providing a leaflet or form which sets out what will happen to their confidential information. The document that follows is an example of a form used by one agency to make it clear to service users that information about them will be shared within the agency and sometimes beyond.

The National Brokerage Network

Sharing Information Agreement

I .... give my permission for the NBN Broker

to contact my **General Practitioner, Local Borough Council, Social Care Services, Department for Work and Pensions, Housing Associations and Primary Care Trusts** and any other individual or organisation listed below:

I request that you share information with the NBN Broker.

Signature ....

Name ....

Address ....

....

Date ....

This remains active until further notice.

Signed ....Date.........

The National Brokerage Network is incorporated within the Inclusion Partnership.
Promoting Independence Choice and Control For Disabled and Disadvantaged People
Company No: 05492971

Version2 –NBN 01/2007

Making service users formally sign that they consent to their personal information being shared makes it clear to them this will happen

However, it is important that leaflets like this are not the only way in which care workers try to make sure that service users consent to their information being shared. Individuals may well need more specific information about their own particular circumstances.

Implied consent

Implied consent is when someone has not explicitly said that their personal information may be shared but their behaviour suggests that they are aware that it will be passed on and they are happy with this. An example of this from Unit 2 is when Anwar Malik's GP referred him to the Diabetes Clinic. His GP did not formally ask Anwar if it was all right to pass on personal information about him to the staff at the hospital, and certainly Anwar didn't sign anything to say that he consented to it. But his GP, reasonably, assumed that because Anwar agreed to go to the Diabetes Clinic he also agreed to his information being passed on.

Ideally, service users should give explicit consent before information about them is shared with other staff or agencies. However, this can be very difficult in practice. Sometimes people are unable to give explicit consent. This includes people who are unconscious, or very agitated or confused. It would be impossible to run health and social services if no information could be transferred before an unconscious patient regained consciousness, or unless a person with Alzheimer's disease became lucid enough to be asked permission. In addition, however capable a person might be, it would make health services in particular very difficult to run if consent were required for each and every occasion that records passed from one member of staff to another: hospital doctors, social workers, medical students, GPs, medical records officers, ward clerks, practice managers, agency staff, and so on.

For this reason, within the NHS, it is possible to pass on some types of personal information when the person concerned has given only *implied consent* to their information being shared. This is based on the assumption that people generally know that information about them will be shared in order to provide them with appropriate health care. As long as someone has been made generally aware that information is shared in this way, they are deemed to consent unless their behaviour clearly indicates otherwise. The NHS guidance for England says:

> Patients understand that some information about them must be shared in order to provide them with care and treatment ... Efforts must be made to provide information, check understanding, reconcile concerns and honour objections. Where this is done there is no need to seek explicit patient consent each time information is shared.

> (DH, 2003a, p. 15)

An important principle in the guidance is that of 'no surprises':

> Consider whether patients would be surprised to learn that their information was being used in a particular way ...

> (DH, 2003a, p. 11)

If someone would be surprised, then they do not already know that their information may be shared, and their explicit consent needs to be obtained.

When patients tell something to their GP it is usually assumed that they are authorising that information to be shared with practice nurses, practice managers, receptionists, and perhaps with a range of people in other agencies as well. You may remember that in Section 2 of this unit you saw an example of the mother of a drug user, Dan, who talked to her GP about her worries about her son. She wanted this conversation kept secret from Dan but it might be seen by a community psychiatric nurse (CPN) if her GP referred her on for support. If Dan's mother agreed to the referral, her GP might judge that she had given her implicit consent to the record of the conversation being shared with a CPN.

However, people don't generally expect their information to be shared with researchers, especially not in a way that could identify them as an individual. So if a researcher wanted to look at what parents of drug users need from GPs, they would need to seek Dan's mother's explicit consent before they could look at her record. Similarly, the record of Amy's baby Zac's immunisations might be accessed by other health visitors or by her GP. But it could be passed on to someone collecting information about rates of immunisation in the local area only if it were fully anonymised.

Implied consent does not *formally* apply in social care settings but many agencies do act as if it applies to them too. The growth of integrated electronic care records makes it particularly important that implied consent is not misused because the information these records contain is more complete and comprehensive, as you saw in Section 3.2.

4.3 Carers, relatives, partners and friends

As you saw at the beginning of Section 4 in the example of the person in hospital who lost his voice, service users may want people who are important to them to be told confidential information about them. Of course often this doesn't involve care workers at all – service users simply share whatever they want with whomever they want. But there are many situations where care workers do become involved. In the example, the service user had literally lost his voice, but sometimes people in hospital are feeling too ill to want to talk to friends and family and prefer a nurse or other health care worker to speak to them on their behalf. Or they may be too distressed about a diagnosis or situation to want to talk themselves. In these situations there should not be a problem with care workers passing on confidential information if the service user wants them to and is capable of giving explicit consent. However, there are often particular issues for organisations about giving information over the phone. It can be hard to be sure that the person at the other end of the phone is who they say they are, and someone answering the phone may not have at their fingertips the instructions about what information a service user wants shared with whom. But there are ways round these problems and they should not be used as excuses for withholding information.

Sometimes there are conflicts of interest between service users and their friends and relatives. Carers often feel they need to know details of the condition of the person they care for in order to support them. The NHS guidance for England states that carers may be told information that is essential to the person's care but explicit consent from the service user is required before personal information is passed on to a carer (DH, 2003a, p. 40). Making the distinction between personal information and care needs can be difficult. If someone needs reminding to take the contraceptive pill (a care need) their carer may well deduce that they are sexually active (personal information), something that the person may not have wanted their carer to know.

"As you are the carer, we have decided we can now share this information with you ... we changed David's diagnosis and medication 15 years ago... "

In the fields of drug abuse, mental health and learning disabilities, practitioners often take a hard line in asserting their clients' right to prevent information about themselves being shared with relatives. This is in order to make sure that people with mental health problems and people with learning disabilities have their autonomy as individuals upheld (Slade et al., 2007). This can lead to conflicts of interest between service users and their carers. The former often want independence and privacy from their relatives, while the latter often feel that, although they shoulder the main burden of care, services keep them in the dark:

> We take the bulk of the caring and the worry, we are the ones who cope in the night or who drive miles in the hope he will attend his programme ... We are, or feel, totally excluded from your updates on his condition.

(Quoted in Shepherd et al., 1994, p. 50)

All the major research on the carers of people with mental health problems, for example, seems to show that carers feel information they need is kept from them (Borthwick, 1993; Shepherd et al., 1994; Rethink, 1999; Rapaport et al., 2006). This is despite the fact that the government's Strategy for Carers emphasises carers' needs for this sort of information (Lloyd, 2000).

In practice, although this is nowhere written down as policy, many services behave as if a client had given implied consent for some confidential matters to be shared with carers, partners or other relatives, even to the extent of disclosing a terminal diagnosis to relatives and not to the dying person (Benson and Britten, 1996). However, not all family and friends are treated in this way; for example, same-sex partners may find that they are not included in this sharing of confidential information:

Polari is an organisation working with older lesbians, gay men, bisexuals and transgender people. You can find out more about their work by looking at their website, www.casweb.org/polari

> We have been told stories of health staff denying access to A & E or intensive care to the partners of lesbians and gay men. In these critical and emergency situations people have been denied information that was, or would have been available to family.

(Lindsay River, Director of Polari, personal communication)

Gay men and lesbians who are in civil partnerships may find that they are more often treated as 'family' with whom confidential information is informally shared. However, many gay and lesbian people are not in civil partnerships and heterosexual partners who are not married are frequently treated as 'family'.

4.4 Passing on confidential information without consent

Although keeping personal information confidential is very important, there are some situations in which it may need to be passed on even though the person it concerns does not give their consent. This final section of the unit discusses such situations further.

In the next activity you are going to return to the story of Amy, Brian and Zac at a critical point in their lives. Christine is visiting them again a few weeks later.

DVD

Activity 10   Can this be kept confidential?

Allow about 10 minutes

Amy confides in Christine and doesn't want her to tell anyone else. What should Christine do?

Find Block 5, Unit 18, Activity 10 on the DVD.

Comment

It was a difficult judgement to make, but on balance I thought that Christine should pass the information on. When you listened to the audio recording you heard that this is what she did in the end.

So this is one situation where the worker judged that information could not be kept confidential, even though one of the people involved wanted it to be and thought she was telling the information 'in confidence'.

Technically, confidentiality nearly always applies to an agency, not to an individual worker; anything a service user tells to a worker in confidence can (and should) be passed on to the worker's line manager or colleagues if necessary. In Christine's case, she discussed it initially with a colleague who has particular experience in child protection issues and then later she discussed it with someone with formal responsibility within her organisation. However, service users are seldom explicitly told this and may assume that confidential information will not go beyond the particular worker. Ideally, Christine would have made this clear to Amy when they first met, as well as having a general conversation with her about how she wanted her information shared. But, as often happens, she didn't do this, perhaps because, as she said in the video scene you saw earlier, she didn't expect there to be any problems with this family. This is one of the reasons that the painful scene occurs.

There are some general principles about when confidentiality can be breached without consent. If a court of law demands that a confidence should be breached, then care workers have no choice but to obey. The most important general principle is that confidentiality should be breached if more harm will be done by maintaining it than by breaching it. So, for example, in the story about Amy and Zac, more harm would be done by leaving Zac in a situation where he was at risk of harm, than by breaching Amy's desire for the information to go no further. Christine's duty of care to children means that she has a particular responsibility to intervene in Zac's best interests. But she was also concerned about the harm to Amy of staying in an abusive relationship. Amy begged Christine not to intervene but even adults can't legally consent to being abused, so Christine would probably have been right to breach her confidence even if Zac were not involved.

Judging when it is justified to breach a confidence is nearly always very difficult. It is important that care workers do not make such a decision on their own, but discuss it with a line manager or other specified colleague. Professional bodies such as the Nursing and Midwifery Council and the General Social Care Council have guidance about this issue. Individual organisations will also normally have guidance that workers and volunteers should refer to.

In addition to these general principles, different organisations have different policies about breaching someone's confidence if they are at risk of seriously harming themselves. For example, employees of prisons and hospitals are often required to report it if they are told that someone intends to commit suicide. By contrast, the Samaritans (the telephone helpline for people who are desperate and suicidal) have an opposite policy. They take the view that people have the right to commit suicide if they wish to and that their role is not to prevent them:

> You do just have to listen, sometimes for hours while the person is dying of an overdose or bleeding to death at the end of the phone, and knowing that if you dialled 1471, you could probably trace the call, and alert the emergency services and save their life. But if the person doesn't want that then that's their right. That's how Sams do it.

(Samaritan volunteer)

So whether someone's confidence that they intend to harm themselves will be passed on depends on the agency involved.

Working with confidential information often involves making very difficult decisions about whether someone has consented to their information being shared or, if they have not, whether more harm would be done by keeping the information confidential than by passing it on. In Unit 20 of this block you will explore these issues in more detail.

Key points

- Best practice is always to make efforts to explain to service users what information collected about them will be used for, and with whom it is likely to be shared.

- Keeping personal information confidential is a vital part of working in health and social care.

- In some circumstances personal information cannot be kept confidential.

Conclusion

In this unit you have looked at record keeping in health and social care settings, especially records about service users. On the face of it, record keeping sounds like a rather dull aspect of care work but you have seen that people can have very strong feelings:

- Care workers complain that keeping records takes them away from the parts of their job that they really want to do.

- Service users and the public at large get incensed if mistakes are made in records or they are lost.

- Service users can find the records that are kept about them frustrating, threatening or upsetting.

- But being able to see their own records can also make service users feel empowered and in control of their own care.

- If information from records is not shared, this can frustrate service users.

- If personal information that a service user wants to be kept confidential is recorded and passed on, this can be extremely distressing – even if it is necessary.

- Having to make the decision to break someone's confidence can be traumatic for care workers too.

Like so many aspects of care work, record keeping is actually all about people, their relationships and their feelings. Using records, whether as a service user or as a care worker, involves dealing with those feelings and relationships as well as the more practical task of making a record that is suitable for its purpose.

These were the core questions that were asked at the beginning of the unit:

- Why do we need personal records in health and social care?

- Why is keeping good records a skilled and important part of care work?

- What difference does it make when personal records are kept electronically?

- In what circumstances should personal information about a service user be shared with other people?

You have seen that personal records play a significant role in making care safer. They mean that a service user's history and past care are not forgotten and this can prevent inappropriate or dangerous care being provided. Personal records can be a way of informing service users of what care they can expect, enabling them to make their own checks about whether they are getting the right services. Sharing information from personal records means that care can safely be provided by several people and several different organisations. Sharing information from records also means that service users who are at risk of abuse can be identified and supported.

Keeping good records is skilled because it is as much about working with people as any other part of the job. It is also skilled because accurate, relevant, up-to-date records do have to be kept. As you will see in Unit 19, keeping records is one way that care workers are made accountable for their actions: if they don't keep good records they can be penalised. Care workers have to continually make choices about how they work with records. Do they keep better records or devote more time to relating to service users? Do they write in abbreviations in order to spend less time creating records or do they spend more time on the paperwork so that it is easier for service users to understand what they have written? There are no right answers to these dilemmas. They require the judgement and ability to negotiate priorities that are such important skills for all care workers.

Computers and the internet can make personal records more accessible to many service users. This can help to equalise the power relationship between service users and care workers. But electronic records may further exclude service users who can't get access to computerised information. Security breaches of computerised records can have much bigger effects and involve much larger numbers of people than if records are paper-based.

Information about individual service users frequently needs to be shared beyond the person or agency that originally made the record. This can be done most straightforwardly when service users are able to give their consent. But it can also be done if more harm would result by not passing on the information than by keeping it confidential.

Learning skills: Getting used to academic writing

As you have worked on K101, you have read articles in the Reader that are written very differently from what you might read in newspapers or novels. And in your assignment essays you have been writing in a way that is quite different from how you might write a letter, say. It is a more formal way of writing. But why are 'academic' articles written in that way? And why are you asked to write in that way in your essays?

Reader

Activity 11   What is the point of academic writing?

Allow about one hour

Jot down a few notes in answer to these questions:

- How would you describe the 'academic' way of writing? What are its special qualities?

- What is the point of writing in the 'academic' way? What does it achieve?

It is useful to think about these questions and try to get some answers because it will help you in your studies, both in reading and, more importantly, in writing.

Now, with your notes alongside, read Section 4.3 of Chapter 4 of *The Good Study Guide,* pages 82 to 89. Its title is 'Why do they write that way?' It explores the distinguishing features of academic writing and the purpose they serve. It discusses why argument and debate are central – the role of criticism and analysis – and the importance of evidence, objectivity and precision. These are all things that you have been asked to aim for in your essays in one way or another, although not in such formal terms. They are not all that easy to grasp and they take a long time to achieve in practice, but reading about them will help you to get a better sense of what you are aiming for.

As you read, make elaborations and revisions to your notes on the questions above.

Comment

This section of *The Good Study Guide* gives you a lot to think about. It may not all have 'clicked' for you on first reading. Nevertheless, it is valuable to have a first run at it and take what you can for now. You can come back from time to time, later in your studies, to read it again and think about these core 'tools of the academic trade' that lie at the heart of university-level study.

The main focus of this unit was on personal records about service users. I hope you can now see that they can play an important role in making care safer. In Unit 19 you will continue to look at safety as you explore some of the ways to assess how best to provide care and support to people who need it.

End-of-unit checklist

Studying this unit should have helped you to:

- explain why keeping records is important in modern health and social care settings
- discuss some of the dilemmas created by keeping records
- discuss some of the advantages and disadvantages of electronic service user records
- explain why sharing personal information appropriately is important
- describe the circumstances in which personal information can be passed on to other workers and agencies.

Unit 19

Getting care right

Prepared for the course team by Rebecca Jones

Contents

Introduction

In this unit you will be looking at some of the different ways in which service users and care workers can make sure that safe and effective care is provided. As you have seen already, health and social care is very complex and decisions about how services are provided can have huge effects on people's lives. In Unit 7 you saw how the change from living in large institutions such as Lennox Castle to living in much smaller, more homely settings had a huge impact on the quality of life of people with learning disabilities. You also saw how the arrival of a new family support worker who spoke Bengali meant that Mina Ali (in Unit 10) finally got the correct diagnosis of her health problems. You may also remember Mick Mason and Owen in Unit 5, the young men with haemophilia who contracted HIV as a result of receiving contaminated blood. They received care which was clearly unsafe and which had enormous effects on the rest of their lives. All of these people experienced huge changes in their lives as a result of the care they received.

Because health and social care can have such significant effects on people's lives, it's imperative that the care that is offered has the best chance of benefiting service users and not harming them. People expect the care services they use to help them. They don't want to have a treatment or receive a service that isn't going to make things better for them, let alone one that might make things worse. But how do you know what the best thing is to do? There are many different treatments, interventions and services available – different drugs for health problems, different types of talking therapy for mental health service users, different ways of receiving services such as traditional home care or Direct Payments. So how do you know what the best option is? How do you make sure that care is not harmful? How can care be provided that is likely to be effective and to work in the way that service users need? How can we make sure that health and social care workers have good reasons for the decisions they make? In this unit, you will look at some answers to these questions.

The first section of this unit looks at what it's like to be accountable as a worker and how accountability contributes to making sure that good-quality and safe care is provided. One important way in which care workers are made accountable is by asking them to follow guidelines and protocols about what to do in particular situations. The second section therefore examines working with protocols and guidelines and the effects they have on the safety and quality of care. The third section introduces you to one currently popular way of finding out the best thing to do – by looking at research evidence of effectiveness. You will explore some of the benefits and limitations of using this approach to making decisions about care. People often use the internet to find out about what sort of care might be best for them. The final section therefore looks at the role of the internet in making care better and safer.

Core questions

- How is it possible to work out what care is likely to benefit service users most?

- What does it mean to be accountable?

- Why have guidelines and protocols become more common and what effects do they have on care workers and service users?

- What is 'evidence-based care' and what are its benefits and limitations?

- How is access to the internet changing health and social care?

Are you taking the IVR?

If you are studying K101 as part of the Integrated Vocational Route (IVR), don't forget to check your VQ Candidate Handbook to see which Unit 19 activities contribute to your electronic portfolio.

1 Being accountable

In Unit 18 you looked in some detail at record keeping in health and social care. Keeping records about what care has been provided is one of the main ways in which care workers are made *accountable* for their behaviour. Being accountable means that you must be prepared to describe and justify your actions to others so that they can judge whether you have fulfilled your duties adequately – you have to give an account of your actions. It also implies that if you are not able to do this, you or the organisation you work for will be held responsible and perhaps incur penalties (Checkland et al., 2004). Making workers and organisations accountable is an important way of making care safer.

People often think about accountability as being about paperwork – filling in forms to record what you have done and why you did it. This is an important part of modern accountability processes (Tuohy, 2003), but there are also other ways of being accountable. For example, when I was visiting a relative in a care home the other day she rang her bell to ask for a cup of tea. Nobody came for half an hour and when the care assistant did arrive my relative said, 'I've been ringing my bell for half an hour, what *have* you been doing?' The care assistant apologised and said that she had been helping another resident who wasn't feeling very well. If you look again at the definition above you can see that this is a form of accountability because the care assistant felt obliged to justify her behaviour. My relative didn't have a lot of power to impose penalties on her – certainly not compared with the power that a line manager or care homes inspector has – but she could have complained to the manager of the home or to a visiting inspector. In this sense she did have some power to hold the care assistant responsible for her actions. So accountability isn't just about keeping records, although that is perhaps the most obvious way in which people are made accountable in modern health and social care settings.

1.1 Who is accountable?

You are going to begin thinking about accountability by looking at a particular situation and working out who is accountable for what goes on. You'll do this by applying some general guidance from the General Social Care Council (GSCC). This guidance applies to everyone working in social care in all nations of the UK. Similar guidance applies to people working in health care; for example, you can read the Nursing and Midwifery Council's advice (Nursing and Midwifery Council, 2008).

Guidance for social care workers

As a social care worker, you must be accountable for the quality of your work and take responsibility for maintaining and improving your knowledge and skills.

This includes:

6.1 Meeting relevant standards of practice and working in a lawful, safe and effective way;

6.2 Maintaining clear and accurate records as required by procedures established for your work;

6.3 Informing your employer or the appropriate authority about any personal difficulties that might affect your ability to do your job competently and safely;

6.4 Seeking assistance from your employer or the appropriate authority if you do not feel able or adequately prepared to carry out any aspect of your work, or you are not sure about how to proceed in a work matter;

6.5 Working openly and co-operatively with colleagues and treating them with respect;

6.6 Recognising that you remain responsible for the work that you have delegated to other workers;

6.7 Recognising and respecting the roles and expertise of workers from other agencies and working in partnership with them; and

6.8 Undertaking relevant training to maintain and improve your knowledge and skills and contributing to the learning and development of others.

(Source: General Social Care Council, 2002)

Activity 1   Who is accountable for what happened?
Allow about 15 minutes

Now think back to the story of Marie O'Brien's first two days at work at Millstream Court, which you read in Section 2.1 of Unit 17. There is a reminder of what happened below. Reread the story, and then look again at the guidance from the GSCC about social care workers' accountability. Make some notes about who is accountable for what happened and which clauses from the guidance apply to them.

Marie O'Brien

Marie works in Millstream Court, a supported-living service for people with physical and learning disabilities run by a voluntary organisation.

[…]

Before her first shift, she went to meet some of the other workers, especially Joan, the senior care officer who would be her team leader. Joan introduced her to Richard and Fakhra as Marie was to be their key worker.

For the first week Marie was on day duty, which involved going to the young person's flat and getting them up, then helping them eat breakfast. On her first day she worked with Joan to help Fakhra get dressed. Fakhra needed a lot of help and, when breakfast arrived, Marie realised that she did not know how to help Fakhra eat. She looked round for assistance but her colleague had already left to help someone else, so she 'owned up' to Fakhra, who grinned. When Marie put the food in too quickly Fakhra spat it out, but gradually Marie found the right speed and relaxed, and they seemed to be getting on well. Nevertheless, Marie wondered if there were specific skills she needed because sometimes the food went down the wrong way and twice Fakhra choked. Marie was afraid that she might accidentally hurt Fakhra despite doing her best.

[...]

On her second day, Marie was to get Richard up first. Richard had his own room and Marie knocked and went in. Joan had said Richard needed 'total care' but Marie wasn't quite sure what that meant. She knew he liked to work and play on his computer using a probe he wore around his forehead. She had been told that he could move from the bed to his wheelchair but would otherwise need help with dressing and toileting.

When Marie went to help Richard get up it was obvious that he had an erection. She didn't know what to do. She wondered if she should go out of the room or go to find Joan, but probably Joan would be busy and also Marie didn't know what she would say, so she decided to stay and just turn away for a bit. Eventually she took Richard to the bathroom. By this stage she was confused as well as embarrassed. She realised that Richard was going to need help to go to the loo and saw the urinal bottles on the shelf. Since he could not use his hands she had to put his penis into the bottle and keep it there while he urinated. Then she took him back to his room and helped him to wash his face and get dressed.

(Block 5, Unit 17, pp. 18–20)

Clearly, what went on was not best practice, even though nothing went disastrously wrong. It could certainly have been made safer. Marie felt quite under-prepared and unsupported. Fakhra choking on her breakfast could have been serious. We don't know how Richard felt about their encounter but he may well have found it embarrassing – we know that Marie was very uncomfortable.

So who was accountable for what happened?

Comment

According to the guidance, Marie was accountable because the following sections in the GSCC guidance apply to her:

> 6.4 Seeking assistance from your employer or the appropriate authority if you do not feel able or adequately prepared to carry out any aspect of your work, or you are not sure about how to proceed in a work matter;
>
> 6.1 Meeting relevant standards of practice and working in a lawful, safe and effective way;
>
> 6.8 Undertaking relevant training to maintain and improve your knowledge and skills ...

(General Social Care Council, 2002)

But I also thought Joan, the senior care officer, was accountable because she is responsible for:

> 6.6 Recognising that you remain responsible for the work that you have delegated to other workers;

> 6.1 Meeting relevant standards of practice and working in a lawful, safe and effective way
>
> (General Social Care Council, 2002)

I thought you could perhaps also argue that Joan was not fulfilling this part of her responsibilities:

> 6.5 Working openly and co-operatively with colleagues and treating them with respect;
>
> (General Social Care Council, 2002)

in the sense that it is not very respectful of a colleague to leave them so unsupported in their first few days in a new job.

The manager who employed Marie in the first place, like the senior care officer, is also accountable under sections 6.6 and 6.1.

In addition, I thought that since Millstream Court is run by a voluntary organisation, the trustees of the charity are ultimately accountable for what happens.

Marie was very new and inexperienced and felt quite powerless, but she was still accountable for what happened. Although the support she gave Fakhra and Richard seems quite everyday and mundane (eating, dressing, washing), it could have gone badly wrong and Marie would have been at least partly responsible. When she took on the job of being a care worker, she effectively agreed to be accountable in this way, even though nobody told her this. If the induction into the job had been better, of course, Joan would have explained to Marie that it was Marie's responsibility to let Joan know if she did not feel competent to do a particular task. Even if Marie knew about her responsibilities without being told, she might still argue that it is rather harsh that she is made responsible for her line manager and seniors not preparing her properly for her role.

But making care workers responsible for recognising when they are not sufficiently trained does have the benefit of encouraging them to take responsibility for their own training needs and to think about their practice. It makes it clear that they have a personal responsibility for their actions and cannot simply pass the buck on to their seniors. It may also help care workers to ask for training and development if they use the argument that they are accountable for their actions and they do not feel properly prepared. Care workers being accountable for their own skills and training helps to make care safer.

Marie is not the only person who is accountable for what happened. Her line manager, the care home manager and ultimately the trustees of the voluntary organisation are also accountable. This is an important way in which frontline care workers are protected and it helps to counterbalance their responsibilities.

So far, you have been looking at accountability mainly in the broad sense of people being responsible for their behaviour. This is an important aspect of being accountable but people are also made accountable in more formal ways. In the next section you will begin to look at these more formal forms of accountability and how they relate to informal and personal types of accountability.

1.2 What's it like to be accountable?

In the next activity, you hear someone talking in depth about what it's like to be accountable. Isabel works for a Women's Aid organisation, a voluntary group that provides services to women and children experiencing domestic violence. She works in a refuge that provides temporary housing and emotional and practical support. As the DVD explains, because of the nature of Isabel's work, her family name and the name of her organisation are not specified.

DVD

Activity 2   Being accountable

Allow about 30 minutes

Find Block 5, Unit 19, Activity 2 on the DVD.

Listen to the interview and answer the questions about what it's like for Isabel to be accountable.

Comment

You can see that being accountable is challenging for Isabel. She is accountable to different people (service users, funders, the general public, health and safety authorities) in different ways, and sometimes their requirements are incompatible.

Most health and social care workers are accountable to many different people and agencies, as Isabel is. Isabel is also accountable for her actions in other ways that she doesn't mention here. She is accountable to her line manager and to the trustees of the charity. She is also accountable to legal bodies, such as the courts and tribunals. She is not a member of a profession, but if she were a nurse, a social worker or a physiotherapist, for example, she would also be accountable as a professional. If she did not behave appropriately, she could ultimately be 'struck off' (deregistered) and prevented from working in the area. As you heard in the interview, these multiple accountabilities can create real difficulties for care workers in working out what to do.

Isabel's accountability is both informal and formal. Informally, she is accountable to the service users through activities such as the house meetings and everyday conversations and requests. More formally, she is made accountable by the paperwork she has to fill in for the funders. In the next section you are going to look in greater detail at these more formal kinds of accountability.

1.3 Being made formally accountable

Health and social care workers are made formally accountable for their actions in a variety of different ways. Here are five particularly important ones. For each one I have given some examples from both Marie's and Isabel's situations.

Explicit statements about responsibilities. Both Marie and Isabel have a contract of employment and a job description. Marie's job description states that she is expected to support residents in becoming as independent as possible. If she consistently did things for Richard or Fakhra that they were able and willing to do for themselves (because it was quicker, for example) she could be made accountable for this behaviour by referring to her job description. After she had been in the job for a few weeks, Marie found another source of explicit statements about her responsibilities – a set of guidelines in the staff handbook which covered things such as what to do if a resident had a fit, and safety issues to remember if arranging a holiday for a resident. Isabel also has a series of guidelines and protocols that tell her what to do in particular situations; for example, whom to inform if she is seriously worried about the safety of one of the residents or their children. You will see an example of one of Isabel's guidelines in Section 2 of this unit.

Procedures to make performance or outcomes visible. Both Marie and Isabel have to keep a record of the support they have provided. At Millstream Court, each resident has a care record where Marie has to note down what help she gives. If she forgets to give Fakhra her breakfast or her medication, this will be visible on the care record. Isabel spends some of her time helping residents get the benefits to which they are entitled as quickly as possible. How quickly Isabel manages to do this is monitored.

Penalties for poor performance (and rewards for excellent performance). If Isabel's organisation has empty rooms for too long a period it is financially penalised by its funders. One of Isabel's responsibilities is to try to make sure that rooms are reallocated quickly so that this doesn't happen. Both Marie and Isabel could be disciplined or even sacked for failing in their duties. And if they did something criminal or seriously wrong, they could be prosecuted or sued. They might also be rewarded if they perform excellently: they might receive a bonus or be promoted.

Official mechanisms for examining performance. Once Marie had been in the job for a month, she had a review meeting with Joan to discuss how she was doing. After six months she had a more formal review meeting with the manager of the home. For this meeting, Joan, Fakhra and Richard were all asked to provide feedback on Marie's performance. Isabel's organisation has yearly meetings for service users where an independent facilitator asks them about their experiences of using the services.

Processes for investigating when things go wrong. Both organisations have a complaints procedure which residents can use. If a manager received a complaint about Marie or Isabel this would start off an investigation into what had happened. Both organisations also have a grievance and disciplinary procedure which can be used if other staff have a serious complaint about Marie's or Isabel's behaviour or performance.

These are the sorts of ways in which people are made formally accountable for their actions. In the next activity, you are going to apply this to your own situation.

Activity 3   How are you accountable?

Allow about 15 minutes

Spend a few minutes thinking about a situation in which you are held personally accountable for your actions. If you work or volunteer in a health and social care setting you might like to take that as your example. If you work in another type of setting, you could think about that. Or you could think about family relationships or friendships in which you find you end up explaining and justifying your actions. Then, using the list above, write down which of these types of accountability apply to your situation and what form they take:

- Explicit statements about responsibilities
- Procedures to make performance or outcomes visible
- Penalties for poor performance (sometimes rewards for excellent performance)
- Official mechanisms for examining performance
- Processes for investigating when things go wrong.

Had you thought before that the things you wrote down were part of your accountability?

The aim of doing this activity was to help you think about the day-to-day ways in which you are made accountable for your actions. What you have written will depend on the context you had in mind. If you thought of a work setting or a fairly formal type of volunteering, you probably had examples for most of these headings. But if you were thinking of a relationship or friendship it was probably trickier. One of the things that distinguishes formally provided health and social care from informal family care is that accountability is more explicit.

At the beginning of this section I gave an example of relatively informal accountability – my relative in a care home who was unhappy because it was half an hour after she pressed her buzzer before a worker appeared to give her a cup of tea. The worker claimed she had been busy helping another resident who was feeling unwell. But what if she were lying? What if really she was enjoying a good conversation with a colleague and assumed that my relative didn't need anything urgently? That is certainly what my relative thought was going on. Since this was a fairly informal type of accountability it is unlikely that anybody will ever find out whether the care worker was telling the truth. Few care homes make their workers account for their activities at this level of detail. But forms of care that are considered to be more important are monitored more formally. For example, if my relative had requested painkillers, then the care worker would have recorded the medication she gave her on a special form. If she made any mistakes in what she gave out she could be held accountable for it.

You have heard Isabel talking about how her accountability to the service funders pulls her away from direct work with the residents. And you may remember from Unit 18 that care workers often complain about how much time they have to spend on record keeping. Many of these records are part of what makes workers accountable for their actions. But the danger with creating a lot of formal accountability structures is that care workers end up spending more time and energy documenting their activities, rather than building relationships with service users and providing the best-quality care.

1.4 Creating real accountability

Making sure that care workers are offering good-quality and safe care is undoubtedly very important. What forms of accountability might work best? How can we create real accountability in care services?

One important answer is: by genuinely involving service users in the planning and delivery of care services. The Social Care Institute for Excellence (SCIE) commissioned a report from service users about what they wanted for the future of adult social care (Beresford et al., 2005). (You will learn more about SCIE later in the unit.) One of the things the authors discuss is the importance of service providers and workers being accountable to service users for the way they provide services. They emphasise that it is essential that service users are involved in service delivery at every stage, from planning, through implementation, to review and monitoring.

Another way of creating real accountability is by increasing individual service users' access to knowledge. As you will see, the internet plays a role here for some people, and the Freedom of Information Act 2000 can also be used to empower service users. Individuals can find out most of the information that an agency keeps about its performance and can use this to inform their own situation. For example, parents-to-be can find out the Caesarean rate at local hospitals to help them make a decision about which hospital to go to. Organisations can also make efforts to pass information on to service users and make sure that it is available in accessible forms.

Real accountability can also be created by the way in which care workers act. They can listen carefully to what service users tell them about their needs. They can try to prioritise service users' interests over 'what is usually done' or what is most straightforward to arrange. They can try to reduce the power imbalance between themselves and service users by sharing information and by being honest about the dilemmas they face (George, 2003; Checkland et al., 2004).

One of the most effective ways of creating real accountability is by changing lines of responsibility. For example, a user of Direct Payments becomes the employer of the person who is supporting them. This means that the care worker becomes accountable to the service user for their behaviour and actions. If the service user is unhappy about the way care is delivered, the care worker cannot claim that they have to do things in a particular way because their line manager says so. Instead, they have to justify and account for their actions directly to the service user. This is in marked contrast to a traditional home care service where the worker's strongest lines of accountability are to their manager and employing organisation. Some voluntary organisations are controlled by the service users or have a high percentage of service users in their management structure, and this too can help to create real accountability.

Although creating real accountability is challenging, it can be done. It is in everyone's interests to ensure that there are good ways of making care workers accountable for their actions. Care workers being held accountable for their actions plays an important role in making care safer.

Key points

- Being accountable means that you have an obligation to describe and justify your actions to others so that they can judge whether you have fulfilled your duties adequately.

- Health and social care workers and organisations are accountable to many different people and agencies. This can lead to conflicts of accountability.

- People can be made accountable quite formally through paperwork and procedures or more informally through everyday conversation.

- Real accountability can be increased by involving service users in the management, design and evaluation of services, and by care workers acting in empowering ways.

2 Working with protocols and guidelines

One of the ways in which Marie and Isabel are made accountable for their practice is that they have to follow guidelines which tell them what to do in particular situations – for example, if a resident has a fit or if there are serious worries about someone's safety. You have already read about guidelines for record keeping in the previous unit. In this section you will look in more detail at protocols and guidelines and you will consider whether they do help make care better and safer – whether they contribute to getting care right.

2.1 Introducing protocols and guidelines

The box that follows contains an extract from the guidelines about child protection at Isabel's organisation.

Child protection guidelines at Women's Aid

8   If a child discloses abuse to a member of staff or a volunteer

8.1 Women's Aid staff or volunteers will:

- Stay calm and listen carefully.

- Reassure the child that s/he was right to disclose what happened and that the abuse is not her/his fault.

- Explain to the child that in these circumstances confidentiality cannot be maintained.

- Assure the child that the issue will be taken seriously.

- Fill out an incident form immediately stating what was said by both the child and the member of staff, and recording facts rather than opinions.

- Discuss this with the member(s) of staff responsible for dealing with child protection issues, decide on the appropriate course of action and record this decision.

8.2 If the abuse is recent or continuing, staff or volunteers will also

- Tell the child what action is likely to be taken, who will be informed and what the consequences may be.

- If the child has sufficient understanding, discuss options realistically, including talking with the mother/carer with a staff member present (if the mother/carer is not the abuser).

- Keep the child informed throughout the entire process.

8.3 The staff member will then discuss the allegations with the designated
person or child protection team, who will decide on a course of action
depending on the nature and seriousness of the abuse and consult
with Children's Services at the earliest opportunity regarding whether
a referral to Children's Service is needed.

(Source: Personal communication)

This is one section from a larger set of guidelines which tell Isabel how to
proceed if she has worries about the safety of a child. As you have seen, this
particular section tells her what to do if a child lets her know that they are being
abused. The guidelines contain general advice on how to behave (e.g. 'stay calm
and listen carefully', 'reassure', '[record] facts rather than opinions') as well as
specific steps to take (e.g. 'fill out an incident form' and 'discuss this with the
member(s) of staff responsible for dealing with child protection issues, decide
on the appropriate course of action and record this decision'). Isabel can refer
to these guidelines to check that she has done everything necessary. Written
instructions like these can be particularly useful when dealing with an upsetting
issue like possible child abuse. The guidelines also are one of the ways in which
Isabel is made accountable for her actions. If, for example, it later came to light
that she had not filled in an incident form or she had not discussed it with her
colleague, she could be disciplined.

A protocol is another term for this sort of guidance. It is more often found in
health care settings than in social care organisations. It is sometimes used to
describe quite detailed step-by-step instructions or rules by which organisations
agree to be bound. However, a study examined how people used the different
terms for this sort of guidance and found that the terms 'protocol', 'guideline',
'guidance' and 'pathway' were all used interchangeably in different contexts
(Ilott et al., 2006). For the purposes of this unit the distinction between protocols
and guidelines does not matter.

Guidelines and protocols tell you what to do in a particular set of circumstances.
They are designed to standardise some aspects of care in order to improve care
outcomes and make care safer (NHS Modernisation Agency/National Institute
for Health and Clinical Excellence, 2002). They formalise the ways in which
health and social care workers are supposed to carry out their jobs. Of course,
there have always been procedures and instructions within workplaces. But
from the 1990s onwards there has been an increased emphasis on formalising
everyday work into guidelines and protocols. There has also been more
emphasis on making care workers accountable for whether they have followed
their guidance.

Protocols and guidelines make it possible for staff to undertake more complex
tasks. So, for example, many home carers nowadays change catheter bags.
Traditionally, this was a task for nurses but protocols have been written which
detail the process to be followed and the problems to look out for. This makes it
possible for home carers to change catheter bags safely without having specialist
nursing knowledge. And this in turn gives district nurses more time to work with
service users who need more complex care, enabling people to stay at home
rather than going into hospital or into residential care.

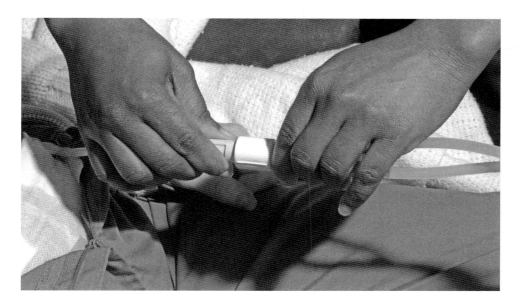

Home carers can safely change over catheter bags because they have access to written protocols which tell them exactly what to do

2.2 Where do protocols and guidelines come from?

Protocols and guidelines can come from a wide variety of sources. They might be specific to a particular organisation, like Marie's guidelines about how to arrange a holiday for a resident. They might come from a primary care trust, or from national organisations such as the National Institute for Health and Clinical Excellence (NICE) or the Social Care Institute for Excellence. Isabel's guidelines about child protection come mainly from the national organisation Women's Aid, with minor changes to fit the situation of her particular group. Professional bodies such as the Royal College of Nursing also provide guidelines. These organisations examine different forms of evidence about what works best. They look particularly for research evidence of what is generally effective (you will discover in more detail what is meant by basing care on evidence in Section 3). But they also look at other forms of evidence such as what service users say about different forms of care and what care workers have found.

People giving advice on how to create protocols and guidelines usually emphasise the importance of involving service users in the development process. One guide warns:

> If this does not happen, professionals will make assumptions about what patients want and need or pay little attention to the issue. The result is likely to be service-focused, shaped to meet the needs of the organisation.

(Shuttleworth, 2003, p. 16)

This can be quite difficult to do in practice (Forbes et al., 2001). Service users who have been involved in this sort of development work say that they often encounter problems which make it difficult or impossible for them to be involved (Branfield and Beresford, 2006). Inaccessible venues, inconvenient and long meeting times, lack of pay, long timeframes for projects, and feeling that their presence is only a token can put service users off being involved.

These problems mean that, in practice, protocols and guidelines more usually come from people working in health and social care than from people using services. The danger of this, as the quote above says, is that they may end up focusing on worker and service-level issues rather than on things that affect patients more directly.

2.3 Working with protocols and guidelines

In the next activity you are going to listen to an interview with Marilyn Francis, who has been a health visitor for many years.

DVD

Activity 4   'It's embedded into my practice'
Allow about 20 minutes

You will now hear Marilyn Francis talking about how she uses protocols and guidelines in her everyday work.

Find Block 5, Unit 19 Activity 4 on the DVD.

Comment

Marilyn says that she uses protocols and guidelines a lot in her work but she is so familiar with them that she doesn't need to refer to them very often. She seems generally quite happy to use them and feels they play an important role in making her practice safer.

You heard Marilyn say that protocols and guidelines have become more prominent over the years that she has been a health visitor. Protocols and guidelines have become much more common in most health and social care settings. They are seen as an important way of making sure that people get the right care and that care is delivered safely. Marilyn seemed to agree that they are helpful. But is she typical? What do other people working with protocols and guidelines think? In the next activity you are going to read about some research into this question.

Reader

Activity 5   Procedures and the professional
Allow about 40 minutes

Read Chapter 20 'Procedures and the professional', by Rebecca Lawton and Dianne Parker in the Reader (pages 163–70). As you read, highlight or underline what strikes you as important.

Then reread the section 'What is the main purpose of protocols?' and make a list of what the respondents said were the main purposes of using protocols and guidelines. You might find it helpful to use the three headings: (a) management benefits; (b) effects on staff; (c) improvements to care.

Comment

This was my list:

(a) Management benefits

- To protect management
- As part of risk management

- To protect against litigation
- To keep insurers happy

(b) Effects on staff

- To enable under-skilled or undertrained staff to be used
- To extend nursing roles
- To train new and junior staff
- To provide staff with support they can use to challenge bad practice by colleagues
- To help team working
- To bring older workers up to scratch

(c) Improvements to care

- To define best practice
- To standardise practice and behaviour
- To define correct practice

You might not think all these are good reasons to use protocols and it's clear that many of the respondents were not happy with these reasons either. I also didn't agree with some of the things they said, such as the assumption that there is a problem with older workers.

2.4 What are the problems with using protocols and guidelines?

In the next activity you are going to think about some of the drawbacks of basing care on protocols and guidelines.

Reader

Activity 6   Drawbacks to using protocols and guidelines

Allow about 20 minutes

Return to Chapter 20 in the Reader, 'Procedures and the professional', by Lawton and Parker (pages 163–70).

Make some notes about the problems and drawbacks that the participants in this research study described. You will find the section 'Problems with protocols' particularly useful, but there are also comments about problems with protocols and guidelines in the other sections of this chapter.

Comment

I was particularly struck by the comment that using protocols de-skills the workforce and makes it possible to cut down on the proper training of staff. I noticed that this is the other side of the coin from the claim that one of the advantages of protocols is that they enable staff to work across boundaries. I was also interested that some respondents say that protocols are being introduced for the wrong reasons – they mention pressure from insurers, the hospital 'covering their butt', and managers being able to blame individuals rather than acknowledge failures in the system. Some people who took part in the study were also worried that protocols limited flexibility and that care became less individualised. Some were also sceptical about the quality of the research on which the protocols and guidelines are based, and made the point that no piece of research will tell you the best way to proceed with every single person. Another point that they made was that protocols might lead to rigid thinking and an inability to think laterally. There were concerns that professional judgement and freedom were being limited.

You have seen that protocols and guidelines are designed to improve the quality and safety of care for service users. However, Lawton and Parker note that:

> Although they were asked directly about the effect of procedures on patient care, only very occasionally was improved patient care volunteered as a motive for the drive to proceduralisation in the NHS.

(Reader, Chapter 20, p. 165)

Several researchers argue that the increased use of protocols and guidelines limits rather than improves service users' choice and control (Fowler, 1997; Rogers, 2002). One commentator argues that:

> A patient may suspect that the doctor is more concerned with putting what is, to the patient, a unique illness into a category allowing the use of a protocol not appropriate to their special needs – an 'off the peg' and not 'tailored' treatment.

(Fowler, 1997, p. 242)

So not everyone thinks that protocols and guidelines always improve the quality of care.

You may have noticed some references to the evidence on which protocols and guidelines are based. For example, Marilyn said that she does find working with protocols and guidelines frustrating when she knows that the research on which they are based is outdated – if new research suggests that they ought to be doing something different from what the guidance recommends. In Section 3 you will look at whether basing care on research evidence does help to improve its quality and safety.

Key points

- Protocols and guidelines are formal sets of instructions about what should happen in health and social care settings. They provide authoritative guidance about what to do in particular sets of circumstances.

- Service users are not often involved in the creation of protocols and guidelines. This can mean that the protocols and guidelines end up focusing too much on what is organisationally convenient and important, and not enough on what service users want.

- The increased use of protocols and guidelines has both benefits and drawbacks.

3 Evidence-based care

Since the 1990s there has been increasing emphasis on making sure that the care offered to service users is based on research evidence that it is likely to help. People who are in favour of this approach claim that it is one of the best ways of making sure that the right care is offered. In this section you will look at some of the advantages and disadvantages of basing care on research evidence and you will consider whether it really does help to make care safer and better.

You have seen many pieces of health and social care research as you have studied this course. Many of the chapters in the Reader are summaries of research. For example, in the last section you read about the results of a research study into the attitudes of people working in the NHS to using protocols and guidelines. And in the previous unit you saw some research into patients' experiences of accessing their electronic records. In Unit 9 you studied some graphs about the effects of poverty on health and well-being – these tables come from research into the income and health outcomes of thousands of people. In a more medical field, in Unit 2 you heard how research into diabetes has completely transformed the life expectancy of people with some types of diabetes.

The importance of research evidence

When someone advocates evidence-based care they usually mean that they give particular weight to research evidence in deciding what sort of care to offer. They may also give some weight to other things such as the values and preferences of service users, professional judgement and experience, and local policies and procedures. But the main point about evidence-based care is that it uses research to help make sure that it will actually benefit service users.

3.1 Benefits of evidence-based care

Evidence-based approaches to care started in medicine, and came to prominence in the 1990s (Sackett et al., 1996). They have now spread to nursing, social work, midwifery, mental health work, public health and many other areas (Lambert et al., 2006).

If you want to find out what research evidence suggests is the best care option, it is worth looking at two websites that summarise a lot of research: The Cochrane Collaboration for health care:

>   www.cochrane.org/index.htm

and the Campbell Collaboration for social care (including education and crime and justice):

>   www.campbellcollaboration.org/index.asp

One way of thinking about why evidence-based care is necessary is to consider what may happen if care is not based on research evidence. Three particularly important problems that may arise are: harm, unnecessary interventions and waste of resources.

Harm. Care that is not based on research evidence may not just fail to work – it may actually harm service users. For example, in health care, 'bed rest' often used to be recommended for a variety of situations, including after surgery, for back pain, for high blood pressure in pregnancy and after heart attacks. It might seem sensible to rest if you have these conditions – after all people often go to bed when they are unwell. However, a review study of research into the effects of bed rest found that not only did it provide no benefit, but sometimes it made things worse (Allen et al., 1999). In a different field, a researcher studied five separate programmes aiming to prevent people who had been convicted of crimes from reoffending (McCord, 2003). The programmes were well designed, appreciated by service users, and used well-respected techniques such as mentoring and education. However, it was clear that the programmes had actually increased reoffending rates. This is not a result that you would expect or that common sense would suggest. Using research evidence helps you to get beyond what you think you know or what everyone assumes is the case.

Unnecessary interventions. Without research, treatments or interventions may be offered which do not actually benefit service users. For example, a very high proportion of first-time mothers in the UK have continuous electronic fetal monitoring (CEFM) while they are in labour – 74% in 2001 (Hindley, 2001). This usually means wearing a tight belt which reduces mobility. But research shows that CEFM is not needed for low-risk pregnancies and it increases the risk of needing a Caesarean or forceps delivery (Vintzileos et al., 1995).

Another example from childbirth is the use of enemas. It used to be routine to give women enemas during labour in the hope of reducing infection, but an enema can be very unpleasant and can cause additional pain. Research shows that it does not decrease rates of infection and is therefore an unnecessary intervention (Reveiz et al., 2007).

Waste of resources. Evidence-based care can also help make sure that resources are not wasted. If research studies have not been done into what care works, resources may be wasted by providing care that does not help. For example, many young children suffer from ear infections and they were often prescribed antibiotics. However, a review of the research evidence shows that most ear infections will clear up spontaneously (Glasziou et al., 2003). Therefore it is a

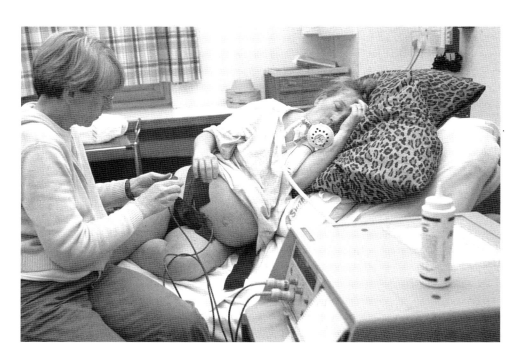

Wearing a belt to enable continuous electronic fetal monitoring limits a woman's ability to move around during labour

waste of resources to routinely prescribe antibiotics for ear infections in young children. In addition, if two care options are equally effective and acceptable to the service user, it may make sense to offer the cheaper one first.

Apart from avoiding problems, there are direct benefits in emphasising the role of research evidence in making decisions about care. Evidence-based care means that care is offered because it is based on research that it works, not because of 'the opinions of others, pronouncements of "authorities", unchecked intuition, anecdotal experience, and popularity (the authority of the crowd)' (Gambrill, 1999, p. 348).

Another benefit of research-based care is linked to service users' confidence in their care. Many service users are less willing to simply trust a professional's judgement these days. They want to know why a particular option is being offered to them and research evidence can provide the explanation.

Basing care on research evidence also helps care workers stay current. It means they don't just rely on what they learned when they were training or in the early years of the job. Knowledge and research are constantly changing and being updated, and workers need to be aware of new approaches and treatments. Practising evidence-based care is one way in which workers can do this.

You may have noticed that many of the examples I have given are related to health rather than to social care. This is because, as stated at the beginning of this section, evidence-based care started in health care and is still more common there. Evidence-based care is increasingly found in social care, but there are more difficulties in basing social care on research, as you will explore in the next section.

3.2 Problems with evidence-based care

As you have seen, evidence-based care means prioritising findings from research when deciding what forms of care to offer. Although many people would agree with offering evidence-based care in principle, once you look at what it means in practice, it is clear that it can be problematic.

What is best in general is not necessarily best for an individual. Research evidence can tell you what is most likely to work but it doesn't tell you whether it *will* work for a particular service user. A particular drug may work for most people but it won't work for everybody. Of course it makes sense to know what is most likely to work. But research evidence only ever tells you about what is *generally* best, never what is best for a particular person.

"Evidence shows this approach works for 90% of service users, unfortunately you are in that stubborn 10% who don't seem to want to benefit."

What works best is not always acceptable to someone. Evidence-based care tends to talk about the 'effectiveness' of a treatment or form of care. How well something works is often the highest priority in making treatment decisions for some forms of medical care – if someone is seriously ill they generally want the medication that has the best chance of making them better. But in other situations, and particularly in social care, it is equally important to work out whether something is acceptable to service users, whether it helps them maintain their dignity and independence, or whether it is appropriate to their particular situation. For example, research shows that older people at risk of falling have fewer falls if they do the right type of muscle strengthening and balance exercises (Gillespie et al., 2003). But a particular older person might think it makes them look ridiculous to do exercises and so be unwilling to do them.

Missing evidence. In an ideal world, there would be good-quality evidence for every possible type of care. However, this is far from being the case.

"According to our evidence base you should either be fully recovered by now, or dead ..."

It is very difficult to design research studies for some types of situations. For example, you might want to find out whether children who have been abused are helped more by individual counselling or by peer support groups. But this is very difficult to assess, even if you have access to two similar groups of children receiving the two forms of support. Factors such as the counsellor or facilitator's personality and skills, the children's personalities and histories, and the group dynamics that build up in a group setting will all affect the outcomes. This means that there is very little good-quality research evidence for complex issues like this. We have much more research evidence about the sorts of interventions that are easier to measure and assess (e.g. the effect of a particular drug on white blood cell counts) and much less about complex cases involving people's personalities and individual situations. But just because something is difficult to assess, it doesn't mean that it is unsafe or ineffective. Several commentators have noted that this is increasingly a problem – evidence-based care has become so powerful that it makes it difficult to offer services that are not clearly based on evidence (Kerridge et al., 1998; Webb, 2001; Little, 2003; Gray and Macdonald, 2006; Lambert, 2006; McNeill, 2006).

It rarely empowers service users. Some research is designed, commissioned or undertaken by service users and this can mean that service users' priorities and interests are addressed (Glasby and Beresford, 2006). However, this is still quite rare and it is mainly professionals who decide what gets researched, interpret the findings and decide what it means for practice (Kerridge et al., 1998). This means that basing care on research evidence is unlikely to empower service users.

The priority given to evidence-based care can make it harder for service users to get the care they want if there is not clear evidence that it is likely to work.

It undervalues care workers' skills and experience. Evidence-based care can leave little room for experienced care workers' skills in assessing complex personal situations. In particular, it does not allow for intuitive knowledge, which is important in some traditions of social care and nursing (Benner, 1984; Davis-Floyd and Davis, 1996; Marks-Maran, 1997).

If you want to know more about these problems with evidence-based care you can read Reader Chapter 28, 'Ethics and evidence based medicine', by Ian Kerridge, Michael Lowe and David Henry (pages 243–7), which looks at some of the ethical problems of evidence-based medicine.

In the next activity you will apply these ideas about the problems with basing care on research evidence to a particular situation – bed-wetting. You met Christine Fuller, a health visitor, in Unit 18; here you are going to read about another of her clients.

Children who wet the bed

Christine has just finished one of her visits to Amy Bird and her son, Zac Peters. She is walking back to her car when she bumps into a mother and child, Ashleigh and Madison Davies, whom she used to see quite frequently when the child, Madison, was younger. She says hello and asks Madison's mum, Ashleigh, how things are going. Ashleigh gets quite upset and says she is at the end of her tether because Madison is still wetting the bed several times a week even though she is nearly eight now. They have quite a long chat. Ashleigh has heard that you can get medication that helps children stop wetting the bed and she has been wondering about asking her GP to prescribe some. Christine suggests that she should visit the GP to check there isn't any underlying problem, but tells her that if there isn't any medical problem you can get special alarms designed to wake the child as soon as they start to pass urine. These actually work better in the long term and have none of the side effects that medication can have.

An enuresis alarm

Christine knows that an alarm is more likely than medication to help Madison in the long term because reviewers have looked at all the research into how to help children stop bed-wetting and have come to this conclusion. The following box shows you the beginning of a summary of this research. It comes from

The Cochrane Collaboration, which, as mentioned in Section 3.1, summarises research findings about health care interventions.

'Nocturnal enuresis' is a medical term for bed-wetting. 'Desmopressin' and 'tricyclic drugs' are types of medication which can help with bed-wetting.

Alarm interventions for nocturnal enuresis in children

Night-time bedwetting is common in childhood, and can cause stigma, stress and inconvenience … Alarms take longer to reduce bedwetting than desmopressin but their effects continue after treatment in half the children who use alarms … Overlearning (giving children extra fluids at bedtime after successfully becoming dry using an alarm) and dry bed training (getting children to go to the toilet repeatedly and changing their own sheets when they wet) may reduce the relapse rate. There are no serious side-effects, which can occur with drug treatment. However, children need more supervision and time from other family members at first. There was not enough evidence with which to compare alarms with other non-drug treatments.

(Source: Glazener et al., 2005)

Don't worry about the medical terminology in this passage. It is a summary of many different pieces of research into treatments to help children stop bed-wetting. The authors have systematically looked for other people's research into this topic and evaluated the quality of that research. They then present the overall picture. Looking at all the research evidence about treatments for bed-wetting indicates that alarms are a better treatment than medication because they work better in the longer term and they have no side effects. So the advice Christine gave is evidence-based. But how might relying only on evidence-based care limit the help Christine can offer Ashleigh and Madison?

Activity 7   How evidence-based care might limit care
Allow about 20 minutes

Think about Ashleigh and Madison's situation. Under the same headings that I used when discussing the problems of evidence-based care, jot down some notes about how limiting the treatment for Madison's bed-wetting to what the evidence suggests should be done (using an alarm) might not be best for them. The headings are:

(a) What is best in general is not necessarily best for an individual

(b) What works best is not always acceptable to someone

(c) Missing evidence

(d) It rarely empowers service users

(e) It undervalues care workers' skills and experience.

Comment

(a) What is best in general is not necessarily best for an individual

Madison might be such a heavy sleeper that she doesn't notice the alarm. It is possible that the medication wouldn't work either – different people respond differently to medication and Madison might be in the small category of children who are not helped by taking it.

"That's not what it says on the web."

and this helps to make them more accountable to their users and to the general public.

Protocols and guidelines. Protocols and guidelines can often be found on the internet, especially those coming from national and professional organisations. For example, if you are interested in the way women are cared for in labour, you can see all the current guidelines of the Royal College of Obstetricians and Gynaecologists on its website (www.rcog.org.uk). This means that individual service users or care workers can check whether the care they are receiving or offering meets these standards and, if necessary, they can then use this information to argue for alternatives.

Research evidence. The internet is one of the best ways of finding research evidence. You have already read about two general sites: The Cochrane Collaboration (www.cochrane.org/index.htm) and the Campbell Collaboration (www.campbellcollaboration.org/index.asp). There is also a wide range of specialist websites which publish information about the research evidence for particular types of care in an accessible and non-technical way (e.g. www.cancerhelp.org.uk). More and more patients go to see their GP armed with evidence from research findings about their treatment options which they found on the internet. You will read more about the effects this has on care in the next section.

Another way in which the internet can help improve the safety and quality of care is through support groups. In Unit 6 you read Chapter 15 in the Reader, which featured health and social care users getting support from online groups. Mutual support and information sharing between people with similar experiences can play a vital role in helping service users to obtain better services.

4.2 The effects of finding information on the internet

In the next activity you are going to look at a study into how using the internet affected one group of service users – people with cancer.

Reader

Activity 8   People with cancer and information on the internet

Allow about one hour

Read Chapter 21 in the Reader, 'How the internet affects people's experience of cancer', by Sue Ziebland and colleagues (pages 171–9). Make some notes in answer to the following questions:

- What were the main reasons the people interviewed used the internet to look for information?
- In what ways did searching the internet help people get the right care?
- How does this study suggest the internet is affecting relationships between patients and care providers?
- Have you ever used the internet to look for information about your own health care needs? When you did the online project earlier in the course you may have looked for health information that was relevant to you personally. How did your experiences compare with those reported in the study?

Comment

The Reader chapter gives a lot of reasons that people with cancer found the internet a useful source of information. They refer to privacy and you can see how this would be particularly useful for conditions that are often experienced as private or embarrassing, such as testicular cancer. They also mention access to information as and when they needed it rather than just when seeing a health worker, and in their own time rather than under the stress of a consultation. The boxes in the chapter show you the other main reasons people used the internet to find this sort of information.

Although the chapter doesn't focus on the question of getting the right care, I thought it was possible to see how searching the internet contributed. If people are empowered by having more information about their situation and possible treatments, they will be in a better position to negotiate with care providers. The chapter also mentions some examples when patients were able to get non-standard treatment which had better outcomes.

The chapter suggests ways in which internet use affects the relationships between patients and care providers. It discusses people using the internet as a way to verify the advice and information they were given by their own health care providers. Having access to information which allows you to check up on the care you are being offered changes the power relationship between a service user and a service provider in important ways, as you saw during your project earlier in the course. The authors, though, note that one benefit of the internet is that this checking can be done secretly, which avoids potential conflict.

The authors also argue that using the internet in this way allows patients to present themselves as competent and 'normal' despite their illness. In Unit 2 you read about the 'sick role' that people often have to take up in order to receive services. This chapter suggests some ways in which the sick role might be changing by making it more common for patients to take an active role in finding out about their care, rather than just accepting what is prescribed for them – a point also made by Shilling (2002).

One course team member added: 'One of the best things about looking for health information on the internet, I find, is that you *get it straight* – no wondering if they think it's best not to let you know. A friend's wife has just been diagnosed with cancer and she was able to find out straight away from cancerhelp.org.uk that there was an 80% chance that she has less than 2 years to live. Which is just what she wanted to know.'

Finding information about their care on the internet can have different effects on service users' relationships with care workers. It can help them to have a more equal relationship with care workers, where they can discuss what is happening to them (Jadad, 1999). Service users also can feel more responsible for finding out about their own care and for sharing the expertise they have gained with others (Ziebland, 2004). Care workers can no longer rely for their authority on being in a particular job role: now they have to demonstrate that they are knowledgeable (Dickerson and Brennan, 2002). Service users can be empowered to challenge the care they are getting if they are not happy with it, but sometimes the information they find is not reliable or not applicable to their particular situation (Lee and Chen, 2005).

4.3 Who uses the internet in this way?

Not all service users have easy access to computers and some have none at all. For example, people who have literacy problems are likely to make little use of the internet. Generally, people who are younger, more educated and wealthier are more likely to use the internet (Gardner and Oswald, undated). However, you may have noticed the reference in Chapter 21 in the Reader by Ziebland et al. to studies which suggest that people in some socially disadvantaged groups may be more likely than the general population to use the web to search for health information. The authors suggest this may be because people in these groups suspect that they are already disadvantaged in their relationships with health workers, and so they use internet resources to compensate for this (Reader, Chapter 21, p. 178).

The interviews on which Chapter 21 in the Reader are based were collected between January 2001 and November 2002. If this study were repeated now it would almost certainly find much higher rates of internet use overall and there might be changes in which groups use the internet. A study published in 2006 found that in countries with high levels of computer use, such as the UK, the largest growth in internet use since 2002 was by people aged over 50 rather than younger people (Pew Global Attitudes Project, 2006). Older people are still less likely on average to use the internet than younger people, but this is changing.

Learning skills: Understanding the difference between 'growth rate' and 'rate'

Were you confused to read that the largest growth in internet use was among older people, yet younger people use the internet more? Can both of these be true?

In fact, it is quite straightforward. In 2002, 72% of young people aged 18–29 were internet users (nearly three quarters) compared with 30% of people aged 50–64 (less than a third). So the proportion of internet users in the younger group was well over twice that in the older group.

By 2005 the figure for the younger group was 89% (close to 9 in every 10 young people). This is an increase of 17%. Meanwhile, the number of internet users in the older group had risen to 67% (about two thirds). This is an increase of 37% – a much faster rise than for the younger group. Indeed, internet use in the older group had more than doubled in just three years. Yet it had still not caught up with usage rates in the younger group.

So there is nothing contradictory about saying both:

- in 2005 UK internet usage rates were highest among younger people

- over the three years leading up to 2005 internet usage was growing fastest among older people.

When you read that the figures for something are growing quickly, it is easy to jump to conclusions that they must have reached a high level. But it all depends where they start from. If you read that the number of cases per year of a disease has doubled, it could mean an increase from 1% of the population to 2%, or it could even be an increase from just one in every hundred thousand of the population to two in every hundred thousand. However, a newspaper headline might make it sound as though half the national population is at risk. Rates of growth and decline are important, but it is always necessary to know what the base figure is in order to judge *how* important.

The key point remains that you can't assume people in particular groups don't use the internet to find information about their care. You might remember that Aerwyn Hall, a young man with learning difficulties whom you met in Unit 3, has a support worker from Somebody Cares who helps him use the internet. Other people who find reading and writing difficult may have a relative or friend who can look things up for them.

In the future it is likely that more and more service users and care workers will find information on the internet as part of the way they try to get care right.

Key points

- Looking information up on the internet can be an important way of improving the quality and safety of care.

- It can change relationships between service users and care workers.

- Not everyone has access to the internet. It is not always possible to predict whether someone will use the internet or not.

Conclusion

In this unit you have looked at some different ways of trying to make sure that service users get the right care – care that will help and not harm them. Care has huge impacts on people's lives: good care can help people become more independent and realise their potential; unsafe or poor-quality care can harm them or reduce their quality of life. So it's really important that care is 'got right'. You have examined four common ways in which people try to do this.

First, you have seen that care workers are accountable for their actions, even when they are very junior and very new to a job. This means that they have to take responsibility for the consequences of their actions, and they can be penalised if their actions lead to poor-quality or unsafe care. More senior workers and managers share this accountability for what happens in their organisations and for the work they delegate to other people. Sometimes care workers are made accountable quite informally through everyday conversation and informal meetings. More obviously, they are made accountable through formal processes of record keeping and performance measuring. This can create tensions for care workers who may feel that time spent accounting for their actions reduces their ability to build relationships with service users and provide the best-quality care. As you saw in Unit 18 in relation to record keeping in general, working out how much detail needs to be recorded is challenging. It is important that care workers are made accountable for their behaviour but it is also important that they do not end up focusing more on documenting their activities than on providing the best-quality care.

Second, another common way in which people try to make sure that care is right is by using protocols and guidelines to formalise health and social care work. These provide a way of making care workers accountable for their actions because it is relatively easy to measure whether someone has followed their guidelines. Protocols and guidelines also mean that busy care workers can provide evidence-based care without having to research all the issues themselves. However, some people feel that the increased emphasis on using protocols and guidelines can reduce the flexibility of care and make it less focused on service users.

Third, evidence-based care can play an important role in making sure that the right care is offered. Although limiting care to approaches for which there is clear research evidence can create difficulties, evidence-based care does help prevent the use of interventions and treatments which are harmful, ineffective or wasteful.

Finally, you have seen that the growth in information and access to the internet means that many service users can independently look for information about different care options. If service users feel empowered by this access to information they are more able to speak up for themselves and make sure that the care they are receiving is suitable for their particular circumstances, needs and desires. Similarly, care workers can use the internet to find out whether the systems and interventions their own organisation offers are generally thought to be good ones.

A theme running through this unit has been the importance of service users' voices being heard. Since service users are predominantly the people who suffer if care goes wrong, it is vital to listen to their experiences about how to get it right. Service users also often perceive things differently from care workers and organisations because their interests can be different. Listening to service users gives a more complete picture of how care is working.

Learning skills: Understanding how learning happens

You have been studying for nearly six months now. I hope you feel that you have learned a lot – that you have many ideas and ways of thinking that were not in your head at the start of the course. But how exactly did they get there? And what use are they to you? To take the second question first, you should now find that:

1   you can make much better sense of discussions about health and social care issues – you have a better grasp of what is being talked about and why

2   you are in a much better position to join in such discussions and to say and write things for yourself.

Higher knowledge takes the form of discourse. Knowledge comes into being when people who have become recognised as 'experts' talk to each other about the world. So access to knowledge is essentially access to discourse. And the aim of K101 is to give you better access to expert discourse on health and social care.

You acquire access to discourse in four basic ways: by listening, reading, writing and speaking. By reading the course units and Reader chapters you have made expert discourse about health and social care 'happen' in your head. And by listening to experts such as David Matthews in Unit 2, Julie Borek in Unit 3, and the many others in subsequent units, you have heard how they discourse about the things they are expert in. In this way you have gradually become more attuned to expert ways of thinking and talking about things. And if you have had opportunities to talk about K101 topics at day schools, or on the phone, then you will also have been able to get practice in speaking health and social care discourse.

But the deepest learning has been when you have written essays. Ideas and ways of thinking really become part of your own mental equipment through taking over the expert discourse and using it for yourself. That is why essay writing is such hard work. You have to struggle to make new ideas work for you. Not surprisingly, it doesn't always come out well, but it is the thinking process that is important, rather than the product. The essay you produce is just a stepping stone: the thinking that goes into it stays with you.

Reader

Activity 9   Different modes of learning

Allow about one hour

You can read more about how you learn as you read, listen, write and speak in Sections 4.4 and 4.5 of Chapter 4 of *The Good Study Guide*, pages 89 to 98. This will help you to think about the challenges you have experienced as you have studied K101. It will also help you to recognise what you have learned. As you read, try to think of examples from your studies on this course.

When you reach Table 4.2 in *The Good Study Guide*, think of an example of something you have read, something you have viewed or listened to, and an essay you have written. See whether you can identify the challenges and the advantages listed. If you went to a day school, or talked about K101 on the phone, you can also think about the contribution that made to your learning.

Comment

The reason it is worth thinking about these things is that you are devoting many hours to learning. The better your insight into the way learning works, the more you will get out of those study hours.

End-of-unit checklist

Studying this unit should have helped you to:

- describe what it means to be accountable as a worker in health or social care, and how accountability helps to make care safer and better quality
- explain why guidelines and protocols have become more important and describe some of the effects this has on care workers and service users
- describe what is meant by evidence-based care and discuss some of the advantages and limitations of this approach
- discuss how service users' access to the internet can contribute to making sure the right care is offered.

References

Allen, C., Glasziou, P. and Del Mar, C. (1999) 'Bed rest: a potentially harmful treatment needing more careful evaluation', *The Lancet*, vol. 354, no. 9186, pp. 1229–33.

Benner, P. (1984) *From Novice to Expert: Excellence and Power in Clinical Nursing Practice*, London, Addison-Wesley.

Beresford, P., Shamash, M., Forrest, V., Turner, M. and Branfield, F. (2005) *Developing Social Care: Service Users' Vision for Adult Support*, London, Social Care Institute for Excellence.

Branfield, F. and Beresford, P. (2006) *Making User Involvement Work: Supporting Service User Networking and Knowledge*, York, Joseph Rowntree Foundation.

Checkland, K., Marshall, M. and Harrison, S. (2004) 'Re-thinking accountability: trust versus confidence in medical practice', *Quality and Safety in Health Care*, vol. 13, no. 2, pp. 130–5.

Davis-Floyd, R. and Davis, E. (1996) 'Intuition as authoritative knowledge in midwifery and homebirth', *Medical Anthropology Quarterly*, vol. 10, no. 2, pp. 237–69.

Dickerson, S.S. and Brennan, P.F. (2002) 'The internet as a catalyst for shifting power in provider–patient relationships', *Nursing Outlook*, vol. 50, no. 5, pp. 195–203.

Forbes, A., Berry, J. and While, A. (2001) 'Critique of a protocol for annual review of older people with diabetes', *British Journal of Community Nursing*, vol. 6, no. 12, pp. 652–9.

Fowler, P.B.S. (1997) 'Evidence-based everything', *Journal of Evaluation in Clinical Practice*, vol. 3, no. 3, pp. 239–43.

Gambrill, E. (1999) 'Evidence-based practice: an alternative to authority-based practice', *Families in Society: The Journal of Contemporary Human Services*, vol. 80, no. 4, pp. 341–50.

Gardner, J. and Oswald, A. (undated) *Internet Use: the Great Divide* [online], www2.warwick.ac.uk/fac/soc/economics/staff/faculty/oswald/bsago12.pdf (Accessed 30 June 2008).

General Social Care Council (2002) *Codes of Practice for Social Care Workers and Employers: Social Care Workers* [online], www.gscc.org.uk/NR/rdonlyres/041E6261-6BB0-43A7-A9A4-80F658D2A0B4/0/Codes_of_Practice.pdf (Accessed 30 June 2008).

George, A. (2003) 'Using accountability to improve reproductive health care', *Reproductive Health Matters*, vol. 11, no. 21, pp. 161–70.

Gillespie, L.D., Gillespie, W.J., Robertson, M.C., Lamb, S.E., Cumming, R.G. and Rowe, B.H. (2003) 'Interventions for preventing falls in elderly people', *Cochrane Database of Systematic Reviews*, issue 3, article no. CD000340 [online], www.cochrane.org/reviews/en/ab000340.html (Accessed 30 June 2008).

Glasby, J. and Beresford, P. (2006) 'Who knows best? Evidence-based practice and the service user contribution', *Critical Social Policy*, vol. 26, no. 1, pp. 268–84.

Glasziou, P.P., Del Mar, C.B., Sanders, S.L. and Hayem, M. (2003) 'Antibiotics for acute otitis media in children', *Cochrane Database of Systematic Reviews*, issue 4, article no. CD000219 [online], www.cochrane.org/reviews/en/ab000219.html (Accessed 30 June 2008).

Glazener, C.M.A., Evans, J.H.C. and Peto, R.E. (2005) 'Alarm interventions for nocturnal enuresis in children', *Cochrane Database of Systematic Reviews*, issue 1, article no. CD002911 [online], www.cochrane.org/reviews/en/ab002911.html (Accessed 30 June 2008).

Gray, M. and Macdonald, C. (2006) 'Pursuing good practice? The limits of evidence-based practice', *Journal of Social Work*, vol. 6, no. 1, pp. 7–20.

Hindley, C. (2001) 'Intrapartum electronic fetal monitoring in low-risk women: a literature review', *Journal of Clinical Excellence*, vol. 3, no. 2, pp. 91–9.

Ilott, I., Rick, J., Patterson, M., Turgoose, C. and Lacey, A. (2006) 'What is protocol-based care? A concept analysis', *Journal of Nursing Management*, vol. 14, no. 7, pp. 544–52.

Jadad, A.R. (1999) 'Promoting partnerships: challenges for the internet age', *British Medical Journal*, vol. 319, no. 7212, pp. 761–4.

Kerridge, I., Lowe, M. and Henry, D. (1998) 'Personal paper – ethics and evidence based medicine', *British Medical Journal*, vol. 316, no. 7138, pp. 1151–3.

Lambert, H. (2006) 'Accounting for EBM: notions of evidence in medicine', *Social Science and Medicine*, vol. 62, no. 11, pp. 2633–45.

Lambert, H., Gordon, E.J. and Bogdan-Lovis, E.A. (2006) 'Introduction: gift horse or Trojan horse? Social science perspectives on evidence-based health care', *Social Science and Medicine*, vol. 62, no. 11, pp. 2613–20.

Lee, B.Y. and Chen, E.H. (2005) 'Health care information provided by internet search engines', *Family Medicine*, vol. 37, no. 5, p. 312.

Little, M. (2003) '"Better than numbers …": a gentle critique of evidence-based medicine', *ANZ Journal of Surgery*, vol. 73, no. 4, pp. 177–82.

Marks-Maran, D. (1997) 'Intuition: "just knowing" in nursing' in Marks-Maran, D. and Rose, P. (eds) *Reconstructing Nursing: Beyond Art and Science*, London, Baillière Tindall, pp. 92–108.

McCord, J. (2003) 'Cures that harm: unanticipated outcomes of crime prevention programs', *Annals of the American Academy of Political and Social Science*, vol. 1, no. 587, pp. 16–30.

McNeill, T. (2006) 'Evidence-based practice in an age of relativism: toward a model for practice', *Social Work*, vol. 51, no. 2, pp. 147–56.

Miettinen, O.S. (2004) 'Knowledge base of scientific gnosis: IV. Knowledge base of scientific gnosis vis-à-vis evidence base of this', *Journal of Evaluation in Clinical Practice*, vol. 10, no. 2, pp. 365–7.

Miles, A., Grey, J.E., Polychronis, A., Price, N. and Melchiorri, C. (2004) 'Developments in the evidence-based health care debate – 2004', *Journal of Evaluation in Clinical Practice*, vol. 10, no. 2, pp. 129–42.

NHS Modernisation Agency/National Institute for Health and Clinical Excellence (2002) *Protocol-based Care: Underpinning Improvement*, NHS Modernisation Agency/National Institute for Health and Clinical Excellence.

Nursing and Midwifery Council (2008) *Accountability* [online], www.nmc-uk.org/aFrameDisplay.aspx?DocumentID=4018 (Accessed 6 August 2008).

Office for National Statistics (2007) *Society: Internet Access* [online], www.statistics.gov.uk/CCI/nugget.asp?ID=8&Pos=&ColRank=1&Rank=374 (Accessed 30 June 2008).

Pawson, R., Boaz, A., Grayson, L., Long, A. and Barnes, C. (2003) *Types and Quality of Knowledge in Social Care (No. 3)*, London, Social Care Institute for Excellence.

Pew Global Attitudes Project (2006) *Truly a World Wide Web: Globe Going Digital* [online], http://pewglobal.org/reports/display.php?ReportID=251 (Accessed 30 June 2008).

Reveiz, L., Gaitán, H.G. and Cuervo, L.G. (2007) 'Enemas during labour', *Cochrane Database of Systematic Reviews*, issue 3, article no. CD000330 [online], www.cochrane.org/reviews/en/ab000330.html (Accessed 30 June 2008).

Rogers, W.A. (2002) 'Evidence-based medicine in practice: limiting or facilitating patient choice?', *Health Expectations*, vol. 5, no. 2, pp. 95–103.

Sackett, D.L., Rosenberg, W.M.C., Gray, J.A.M., Haynes, R.B. and Richardson, W.S. (1996) 'Evidence based medicine: what it is and what it isn't – it's about integrating individual clinical expertise and the best external evidence', *British Medical Journal*, vol. 312, no. 7023, pp. 71–2.

Shilling, C. (2002) 'Culture, the "sick role" and the consumption of health', *British Journal of Sociology*, vol. 53, no. 4, pp. 621–38.

Shuttleworth, A. (2003) *Protocol Based Care*, London, Emap Healthcare Ltd.

Tuohy, C.H. (2003) 'Agency, contract, and governance: shifting shapes of accountability in the health care arena', *Journal of Health Politics, Policy and Law*, vol. 28, nos 2–3, pp. 195–215.

Vintzileos, A.M., Nochimson, D.J., Guzman, E.R., Knuppel, R.A., Lake, M. and Schifrin, B.S. (1995) 'Intrapartum electronic fetal heart-rate monitoring versus intermittent auscultation – a metaanalysis', *Obstetrics and Gynecology*, vol. 85, no. 1, pp. 149–55.

Webb, S.A. (2001) 'Some considerations on the validity of evidence-based practice in social work', *British Journal of Social Work*, vol. 31, no. 1, pp. 57–79.

Ziebland, S. (2004) 'The importance of being expert: the quest for cancer information on the internet', *Social Science and Medicine*, vol. 59, no. 9, pp. 1783–93.

Websites

www.campbellcollaboration.org/index.asp (Accessed 30 June 2008).

www.cancerhelp.org.uk (Accessed 30 June 2008).

www.cochrane.org/index.htm (Accessed 30 June 2008).

www.healthcarecommission.org.uk (Accessed 30 June 2008).

www.nice.org.uk (Accessed 6 August 2008).

www.ofsted.gov.uk (Accessed 30 June 2008).

www.rcog.org.uk (Accessed 30 June 2008).

www.scie.org.uk (Accessed 4 July 2008).

Unit 20

Letting the right people know

Prepared for the course team by Rebecca Jones and Andrew Northedge with material originally written by Roger Gomm

1 Care skills: protecting confidentiality

In this section you will explore the difficult practical decisions that care workers have to make in balancing the potential benefits of sharing information about service users with the need to protect their right to confidentiality. To do this you will examine some fictional scenarios involving the staff and service users of an agency that provides support to drug users. The agency is required to have a confidentiality policy. You will read that policy and work out how it applies to particular cases. But first you need to know about the agency itself.

Narcotics Information and Advice Service

The Narcotics Information and Advice Service (NIAS) is a 'street' drugs agency. This means that people can refer themselves directly by just walking in through the door or phoning. It also accepts referrals from people such as GPs, social workers, health visitors and teachers as long as the person concerned agrees. NIAS offers services such as information about drugs, a needle and syringe exchange, information on how to use drugs more safely, and support for people who want to stop using drugs. It also helps its service users deal with other agencies such as housing services, landlords, the criminal justice service, social services and GPs.

NIAS has seven permanent staff and a number of sessional workers. It has a team of volunteers who usually befriend one or more service users. NIAS maintains two offices five days a week in two inner-city London boroughs and satellite offices one day a week each in two outer-London areas. Each full-time office has an appointments-only system in the mornings, a drop-in service in the afternoons, and one late-night opening. Workers and volunteers also visit people in their homes and in prison.

NIAS is a company limited by guarantee and a charity, and has an unpaid management committee elected at a public annual general meeting. Most of its funding comes from contracts with the health authority and the local authority social services department. Both scrutinised the NIAS confidentiality policy and checked it against their own criteria for contractors' confidentiality policies as a condition of awarding the contracts.

Staff at NIAS work closely with the drug problem team (DPT) in the local NHS trust, which is the main prescriber of methadone (the drug prescribed as a legal alternative to heroin). Not all NIAS service users are in contact with the DPT, and not all DPT service users are in contact with NIAS. Workers at NIAS attend the weekly meetings of the DPT, where decisions are made on whether cases should be dealt with by NIAS, or by one of the community addiction nurses, or both. Matters discussed at the DPT meetings are covered by both the NIAS and the NHS trust confidentiality policies.

DVD

Activity 1   Why is confidentiality important at NIAS?

Allow about 15 minutes

It seems that in NIAS' work a lot of emphasis is placed on their confidentiality policy. In this activity you explore the reasons for this.

Find Block 5, Unit 20, Activity 1 on the DVD.

Comment

As you have seen, NIAS service users may have a number of reasons for wanting to keep information relating to their drug use confidential. NIAS itself as an organisation also needs to keep the right information confidential, in order to be able to do its work.

In the next activity you will familiarise yourself with what the NIAS confidentiality policy covers.

DVD

Activity 2   Getting to know the NIAS policy

Allow about 20 minutes

Now you explore why NIAS' confidentiality policy is so important.

Find Block 5, Unit 20, Activity 2 on the DVD.

Comment

You have now seen how significant the confidentiality policy is for employees and volunteers of NIAS and how important it is that they know and understand it well.

You may have noticed, as you were skimming through the policy, that many of the clauses relate to transfers of information from NIAS to other agencies. Confidentiality within NIAS can be tricky, but it gets even more complicated when other agencies are involved. This is what you will explore next.

1.1 Disclosing information beyond the agency

There are many agencies or people who might at some time or another have an interest in information about NIAS service users. Legitimate requests for information might be received from any of the agencies or people shown in Figure 1.

Whether or not NIAS agrees to supply the information requested will depend on the circumstances and how the confidentiality policy applies to those circumstances. This is what the next activity explores, but first you need to meet two NIAS service users.

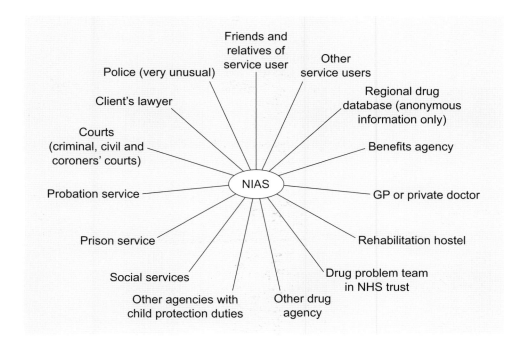

Figure 1 Other agencies and people to whom it may be necessary to transfer information about NIAS service users, with or without their consent

Dan Morgan

You have already met Dan in Section 2.2 of Unit 18. He was trying to find out what his GP had written about his drug use on his GP record, following his mother's disclosures to the GP about him. Dan does not talk to his GP about his drug use, but he does have contact with both the local NHS trust drug problem team and NIAS. As you may remember, he is a heavy user of 'speed', 'which causes him to behave in ways that other people find bizarre' (Unit 18, Section 2.2).

Jonti Igbinovia

Jonti, a friend of Dan's, is a 25-year-old drug user who is being prescribed methadone by the drug problem team of the NHS trust. NIAS is working with Jonti to help him sort out various aspects of his life, such as accommodation and personal relationships.

DVD

Activity 3   Interpreting the policy on disclosure beyond the agency
Allow about 30 minutes

Now try interpreting the NIAS policy regarding circumstances arising in relation to each of these service users.

Find Block 5, Unit 20, Activity 3 on the DVD.

Comment

You now have some practice in applying the confidentiality policy to specific cases. Although the policy looks long and complicated, if you go through the clauses carefully, one by one, you can see that it provides clear guidelines for making decisions on specific cases.

Having explored how the confidentiality policy applies to disclosure of information outside NIAS (clauses 5 to 12), in the next section you will look at how it applies to exchange of information within NIAS (clauses 13 to 18).

1.2 Confidentiality within the agency

For the next part of the case study you need to meet two new characters.

Vicky McDonald

Vicky is a heroin user and referred herself to NIAS after getting to know Dan. She has a three-year-old daughter, Jessica.

Pat Walsh

Pat is a regular volunteer at NIAS. One of her jobs is to be a co-leader for a weekly group meeting, the Wednesday Group, for some of the service users.

The next activity concerns an incident at one of Pat's Wednesday Group meetings.

Dan threatens Jonti

One week Pat was co-leading the Wednesday Group, which included Dan and Vicky, although Jonti, who usually attends, was missing. At one point Dan got very angry about a failed drugs deal for which he blamed Jonti. Dan talked about getting a group of mates together to beat him up. Eventually Pat and some of the group members managed to calm Dan down and move on to other topics.

Later that afternoon, Jonti came to see Pat looking very agitated. He said that Vicky had told him that Dan threatened him and he asked Pat what exactly was said.

Activity 4   What should Pat say?

Allow about 20 minutes

It is time to turn again to the NIAS policy to find out where Pat stands.

Find Block 5, Unit 20, Activity 4 on the DVD.

Comment

You now have a sense of how the confidentiality policy applies to communications between staff and service users within NIAS.

So far you have been looking mainly at protecting individual service users. But, as you saw in the last activity, protection of other people can also be a concern. This is what you explore in more detail in the last section on confidentiality.

1.3 Balancing service user confidentiality against risk to others

You have read already that Vicky has a three-year-old daughter Jessica. Imagine that you are an NIAS volunteer. What responsibility, if any, would you think you have for Jessica's well-being? If you hear things that give you concern about Jessica, should you tell anyone? That is the topic of the next activity.

Activity 5   Concerns about Vicky's daughter

Allow about 30 minutes

Now go back to the NIAS policy to find out your position.

Find Block 5, Unit 20, Activity 5 on the DVD.

Comment

You have now seen how difficult it is to balance the duty of confidentiality against responsibility for preventing serious risk to others.

In fact, where children are involved, the conflicting obligations are particularly difficult to resolve. Suppose, for example, that no one in the statutory health or social services had known about Vicky and Jessica's situation and only NIAS staff knew that there was cause for concern. What steps do you think would be appropriate?

Some drug agencies receive some of their funding from social services and have a contractual obligation to report children who might be 'at risk'. But let's assume that NIAS is not in this position. If NIAS staff are concerned about the welfare of Vicky's child, they should raise the issue with her and try to work with her to provide a safer environment for the child, giving her guidance, for example, on safe management of needles and drugs in the home. But if it seems that Vicky's behaviour continues to put her child at risk, the confidentiality policy (Clause 5b(ii)) implies that NIAS would alert child protection. Vicky would need to be told this (Clause 6), and it is possible that she could be persuaded to

approach social services or a health visitor herself for help with parenting skills. However, recommending that she does so requires a careful estimation of what they are likely to do, and whether it will be to Vicky and Jessica's advantage.

What if the worst happened and Jessica ate some tablets and was seriously ill, or even died? Let's say that Vicky claimed she had been following NIAS guidance on minimising risks to Jessica and the tablets had actually been left lying around unbeknown to her by a visitor. You are then called to give evidence. Would the NIAS confidentiality policy allow you to disclose information in court?

Actually, it doesn't matter what the policy says. If the court requires you to give evidence then you risk being punished for contempt of court if you don't. Also you have to answer questions honestly, or you risk being found guilty of perjury. (Half-truths can count as perjury or as 'obstructing the course of justice'.) A legal requirement to disclose information overrides any duty of confidentiality imposed by your employer.

Key points

- Care workers need to know their employer's confidentiality policy and how to apply it to the cases they encounter.

- Confidentiality codes and policies are not always easy to apply and can raise complex ethical and practical issues – so training and skills development are required.

- Good practice normally obliges a care worker to preserve confidentiality, but there are some circumstances where disclosure is necessary.

- A legal requirement to disclose information will override agency policy.

2 Working with numbers

At the end of every K101 block you have had a DVD activity which explored tables and charts giving facts and figures relevant to care. I hope that, as a result, you now feel well informed about how levels of poverty in the UK changed over the last two decades of the twentieth century and the first years of the twenty-first – and which sections of the population are most at risk of experiencing poverty. I hope you have a good grasp of how, as average life span increases, so does the number of years people are likely to spend in poor health. And I hope you also have a grasp of the related increase in the amount of home care provided by local authorities – although to a smaller number of homes – and of the changing patterns of need for special housing.

All this important knowledge and insight you have gained for yourself, by examining tables and charts. Sets of statistics like the ones you have explored are vital to an understanding of health and social care. Consequently, it is essential that you become comfortable with reading and making sense of the figures that are constantly being gathered to provide a picture of our society and our care services – our characteristics, our needs, the services we use and how we and our lives are changing. To acquire that confident familiarity has, of course, been the underlying purpose of the number skills quizzes on the DVD. Gradually, by working your way through them, listening to the explanations, and then completing the iCMA tasks, you have got to know terms such as axis, median, quintile, trend and blip, and concepts such as percentages and fractions, and how to convert between them, how to identify trends, how to compare different measures, and so on. If, like many students, you had some anxiety at the start of K101 about working with numbers, I hope you now feel a lot more confident. There is much more to learn about how numbers are used, but the essential first step is to recognise how valuable numbers are and to believe that you are capable of making sense of them, if you put your mind to it.

Now it is time to turn to the final DVD activity that deals with number skills.

DVD

Activity 6   How have patterns of living changed in recent times?

Allow about 40 minutes

To explore this question, find Block 5, Unit 20, Activity 6 on the DVD.

Before continuing with this unit, it will be a good idea to complete the iCMA that is flagged at the end of the DVD activity.

Comment

I hope that this final number skills activity has demonstrated once more how interesting and valuable charts and tables can be and that you now feel confident and empowered to explore other tables and charts for yourself.

As we said in Unit 16, you can easily find statistical charts for yourself. Browsing round websites such as that of the UK Statistics Authority (www.statistics.gov.uk) will lead you to a lot of interesting up-to-date information. In particular, you could look on this website for Social Trends, the authority's annual digest of national statistics, which provides headline figures, discussion of what the figures mean and features on particularly significant trends. (You can download a free copy to your computer, to explore at leisure.) Alternatively, just use a search engine such as Google to find statistics on a specific topic and see what comes up. The skills you have developed through the K101 quizzes should have set you up to make sense of a great deal of the material you will find in this way.

3 Learning skills

The main learning skills focus in this unit is on thinking ahead to the K101 exam and getting a very clear idea of what it is all about, so that you can work out a plan and approach it confidently. However, as always, the section ends with a look at how your writing skills are developing.

3.1 Preparing yourself for the exam

In this section you will explore four things to do with exam preparation:

1 You will review the Specimen Exam Papers that you have been sent, to see what pointers they give you in preparing for the real thing.

2 You will review two examples of exam answers so that you get a better idea of what you are aiming to produce in the exam.

3 You will read about the main things that people can get wrong if they approach the exam without thinking themselves into it properly.

4 You will think in more detail about how to revise the course in order to prepare for the exam.

It will take time to cover all this, but it will be extremely valuable in helping you to ensure that you do yourself justice in the exam.

Getting to know the exam paper

You have already introduced yourself to the exam in Unit 12, when you read the section on the exam at the end of the Assessment Guide. Then in Unit 16 you thought about it again, in considering which blocks you might revise. So you know the basic structure of the exam paper. However, there is no substitute for actually looking at a sample paper, so that you can see exactly what you will face in the exam room.

Activity 7 Exploring the Specimen Exam Papers
Allow about 20 minutes

By now you should have received the Specimen Exam Papers. If you have any questions about this, visit the course online forums and ask.

Find your Specimen Exam Papers and read carefully through them, including the instructions.

(a) Make sure there is nothing you don't understand. If there is anything you are in doubt about, ask a question in one of the course online forums.

(b) Notice the three-part structure of the paper – exactly as described in the Assessment Guide. Notice too that you are recommended to spend the same amount of time on each part.

(c) What do you think of the questions? Do they look familiar? Can you see what kinds of answers are needed?

(d) For each paper, read Questions 1 to 5 carefully and underline what seem to you to be the key words. (Use pencil so that you can change your mind later.)

(e) How does looking at the questions make you feel?

Comment

(a) Understanding the instructions on the paper

The paper you get in the exam will look virtually identical to these specimens and will have exactly the same instructions on it. When you are feeling tense, it can be hard to take in instructions. So it's very important to be quite clear now that you understand the instructions and that you ask about anything that seems unclear.

(b) Structure of the paper

As you can see, you are allowed three hours for the exam and you have to answer three questions. All questions are worth the same number of marks, so you should spend roughly an hour on each of your three answers.

You have to choose one question from each of the three parts of the paper. The questions in Part I are on Blocks 1 and 2; the questions in Part II are on Blocks 3, 4 and 5; and the questions in Part III are on Units 21 and 22 in Block 6. This means that you don't need to revise the whole course in detail for the exam. You could focus your revision on just one block out of the first two, one block from the next three and just one of the Block 6 units. However, that leaves you without any choice, so you may want to have some thoughts about your back-up options in case there is a question that doesn't appeal to you.

(c) The types of question

The general form of the questions ought to look pretty familiar to you. They are very similar to the questions asked in TMAs. Obviously, you can't write anything like such a long answer when you have only an hour. But the basic principles are the same, so you should approach your answers in the same way in which you approach TMAs.

(d) Underlining key words

You haven't done your studies for Questions 6 and 7 yet, but Questions 1 to 5 should have rung a few bells for you as you did your underlining. Was it obvious to you that Question 1 was on Block 1, Question 2 on Block 2, and so on? Don't worry if you can't think right now of all that you might want to put in your answers. The main point is to reassure yourself that you can actually make sense of the questions and that you can see how the questions link to the blocks you have studied. Once you start to revise, the key ideas in the blocks will start to come back to you.

(e) Your feelings on seeing the Specimen Exam Papers

Did you find the first sight of the exam papers rather nerve-wracking? Lots of people say they do. Quite a common first reaction is to think that you can't make any sense of the questions at all. But as you underlined key words you should have begun to see that the questions are more or less what you would expect. As you work on the papers during your revision, and develop plans for tackling them, the general structure and format will become a lot more familiar and less daunting.

A three-part paper

The idea behind having three parts to the exam is quite straightforward. Part I gives you an incentive to consolidate your understanding of the early blocks of the course and Part II does the same for the middle blocks. Then Part III provides the opportunity for assessing Block 6. The reason there is no TMA for Block 6 is to avoid distracting you in the period just before the exam.

You can write very good answers in Parts I and II simply by focusing on the block that corresponds to the question number. If it turns out that you can also draw on what you have learned in other blocks, however, that may make your answer even better. But don't feel you have to strive for links across the blocks; just incorporate them if they occur to you. Similarly for Part III: you can stick to Unit 21 for Question 6, or to Unit 22 for Question 7, and write an excellent answer. But you may also be able to bring in material from elsewhere in the course.

Learning skills: Squaring up to the exam paper

As you can see, there is no great mystery to the exam paper. You just write three answers of the same kind that you have been writing all through the course – but shorter. The links between the questions and the course are very clear and you have a choice over which parts of the course to write about. Perhaps you felt apprehensive as you began exploring the Specimen Exam Papers, but now you have had a good look you can see that the exam is fairly straightforward.

Knowing what is expected in answers

You have familiarised yourself with the form and structure of the exam, but what about answering the questions? What is really expected of you? Following the Specimen Exam Papers you will find guidance on tackling them.

Activity 8   Exploring the guidance on the Specimen Exam Papers
Allow about 20 minutes

The first part of the guidance is about the structure of the paper, which you already know about. But there is some very useful information following that.

(a) Read the section on practising answering exam questions.

(b) Read Question 4 on Specimen Paper A. Look at the words you underlined and think for a few minutes about what you might put in an answer to the question. You studied Block 4 quite recently, so what can you remember from the block that could be relevant to answering the question? Just off the top of your head, jot down anything you can think of that could be relevant to an answer.

(c) Now read the guide to answering Question 4 and see whether any of the points you jotted down tally with the notes there.

Comment

(a) There are some useful suggestions in the guidance about how to use the Specimen Exam Papers to practise for the exam – in particular about how to use exam answers to show what you have learned from the course.

(b) How did you get on with this quick stab at approaching a question? Did your mind go blank at first? Or did you find that, having underlined some key words, this gave you a way into thinking about the question? Was Block 4 still fresh in your mind or had a lot of it drifted away? Don't worry if it had – there is plenty of time to get it all back again.

Did you manage to jot some points down? Often just a few scrappy points are enough to get you started on an answer. At this stage, if you were able to write anything that's a bonus. It shows that, even before you have done any systematic revision for the exam, you can come up with relevant ideas for answering a question.

(c) It's hardly likely that you thought of more than a fraction of what is in the notes, because you were tackling this cold. However, perhaps you can see that you had the beginnings of a way into the question – something that you can build on by preparing yourself properly.

Don't read any more of the guidance on the questions just now. Save it for later. When you have done some revision for other questions on Specimen Paper A, you can try the exercise you have just done again. By then you should be able to get quite a lot closer to what is outlined in the guidance.

You have looked at what the 'official' guidance for a question says, but what can students *actually* achieve under exam conditions? In the next activity you can find out.

DVD

Activity 9   Looking at exam answers

Allow about 40 minutes

To explore some exam answers find Block 5, Unit 20, Activity 9 on the DVD.

Comment

This activity will have given you a lot to think about. Since you probably haven't done much revising yet, you may have found it a bit intimidating to see what students are capable of producing under exam conditions and what kinds of criteria are brought to bear in marking. But don't worry, you will quite quickly get yourself tuned up to a high pitch of familiarity with past blocks of K101. The main point is that you now have a realistic picture of what an exam answer is like, so you know what you are trying to achieve. But if you are feeling in need of a bit of reassurance, ask around in the course online forums. You'll probably find that other students are having similar thoughts.

Knowing what to avoid

You now have first-hand experience of what exam answers can look like and an idea of some things that can pull marks for an answer down. You can broaden these insights by reading about the most common mistakes that students make in exams.

Activity 10 Common pitfalls in taking exams
Allow about 15 minutes

Section 12.3 of Chapter 12 of *The Good Study Guide*, pages 343 to 346, summarises what exam boards point to as common faults in exam answers. Read the section now and think about the two answers you have just looked at. You will see pitfalls that the answers avoided, but also ones that they fell into.

Comment

I'm sure nothing you read was much of a surprise to you. It's mainly 'common sense'. But common sense can get forgotten in exams.

Similar comments are made in reports from script markers for courses like K101. They usually remark on how well students have done overall, but identify ways in which some students score less than they should. Here are some common shortcomings that aren't mentioned in *The Good Study Guide* piece you have just read.

Too much description

Some students get bogged down in the details of what they are writing about. They write pages of information about a particular case study, instead of picking out the bits that are really relevant to their argument. You need to give *some* detail to show you know what you are talking about, but if you put in enormous amounts of detail it gets in the way of the argument you are trying to develop in answer to the question.

Not enough critical discussion

To get good marks you usually have to look at two sides of an issue. For example, when a question about life story books asks about their *advantages*, you can usually improve your marks by also considering the *disadvantages*. 'Critical discussion' is taken for granted in degree-level writing.

Too subjective

Some people place too much weight on their own opinions and experience, writing at length about situations the marker cannot make any judgement about. You can bring in your own experience to an extent, but you should never rely on it as your main evidence. You can also bring in your own views as you draw your answer to a conclusion, but don't devote your whole answer to your personal views. Don't expect your script marker to treat you as an authority on the subject. Why should they? Their job is to assess how well you have understood the arguments presented in the course.

Biased

A few students let their own strong feelings dominate their answers. Some launch into political speeches. Some show ethnic or gender prejudice.

Not enough structure

Some answers contain extremely long sentences, or have no paragraphs, or have no beginning, middle and end. Lack of structure makes it difficult for markers to understand an answer.

Poor use of time

Some markers comment on the time a few students waste writing whole pages of immensely detailed plans with lots of crossings out and revisions, when all that is required for an answer plan is a few brief notes. Also there always seem to be one or two students who don't leave time to write a proper answer to their third question, thereby depriving themselves of a large chunk of marks.

Not including material from the course

The most frequent observation, however, is that a small number of students *put hardly anything from the course into their answers*. In the heat of the moment they forget the primary rule, which is *to be sure to include material that is very clearly drawn from the course*.

However, before you get too gloomy, it is important to emphasise that most students don't fall into these traps and actually do very well. Here is what one script marker wrote:

> Overall the performance was impressive. Most students had clearly planned their answers, managed their time carefully and showed a good level of knowledge of the course. Handwriting was easy to read (putting my own to shame!).

So don't be put off by the list of failings. Forewarned is forearmed. If you give yourself time to prepare sensibly and thoughtfully there is no reason why you shouldn't give an excellent account of yourself.

Planning your revision

At the end of Block 4 you wrote down some preliminary thoughts about how much time you would be able to set aside for revision at the end of the course and how you might allocate that time to different revision tasks. Now that you have mulled things over and with the exam considerably closer, this is a good time to revisit the issue and clarify your plans.

> I intend to start by deciding what I am going to revise. Next step – for each block I am going to revise I intend to make notes and gradually reduce them to one page of key notes/diagrams that are meaningful to me. Penultimate step – practise exam questions. Last step – pray and panic!

(Past student)

Reader

Activity 11   Putting more detail into your revision plans
Allow about 45 minutes

Begin by reading Section 12.4 of Chapter 12 of *The Good Study Guide*, pages 346 to 356. This will help to get you thinking strategically about your approach to revision and will give you ideas about the range of tasks on which you could spend your revision time.

Then think about the questions below and make a few notes where appropriate:

(a) Are you going to allow yourself a catch-up week after Block 6, or will you move straight on in order to give yourself more time for revision after Block 6?

(b) Will you wait until you have finished Block 6 before starting your revision, or will you mix revision with studying the Block 6 units?

(c) Unit 23 provides a lot of help with revision, including pre-prepared grids to help you in carrying out systematic revision of your chosen blocks. Should you take a look through the unit first to see what it covers, before getting absorbed in studying Units 21 and 22?

(d) Roughly what percentage of your revision time do you think you will need to give to each of the following?

- Sorting out all your electronic and paper files and course materials

- Going back over your chosen blocks and making notes

- Rereading your essays

- Practising sketching answers to questions, writing out timed answers, making up questions of your own

- Group revising with other students, either online or at day schools.

(e) Do you have a time planner on your computer, such as MS Outlook Calendar? Are you going to use it in planning your revision time? You can either do this onscreen or print some calendar sheets for the weeks ahead.

(f) Work out roughly how many hours you have per block for revision. Mark on your time plan which days you hope to be doing what.

(g) Mark down any day schools or other group revision sessions you have arranged.

Comment

You may find it useful to go back to Section 12.4 of *The Good Study Guide* several times over the coming weeks, to remind yourself what you are trying to achieve.

(a) It's up to you whether you take a catch-up week or not. Once you have submitted TMA 07, you have no other K101 deadlines before the exam. You may feel that time will be more useful to you after Block 6, rather than taking it before and then finding yourself rushed during revision.

(b) Since you are free to manage your time as you like after TMA 07, it may make you feel more confident if you begin some revision straight away. It will also give you a chance to find out what you can achieve in the amounts of time you have available and inject realism into your plans. But be sure not to put off Block 6 for too long, or there won't be time for it to 'sink in' before you have to write about it. Remember that Block 6 is the only one that is compulsory in the exam.

> I haven't done an essay style exam in 28 years. So I've got eTMA 07 out of the way and I'm reading Block 6 and finding it explains a lot. It ties in neatly as a political explanation for the course as a whole. I bought some coloured cards and intend to write down details of the theories and theorists. (I think they'll look pretty.) My kids do this to revise for their exams. They try and get a whole subject on one sheet in note form. I'm a bit scared about writing by hand after so many years.
>
> (Past student)

(c) To a large extent Unit 23 is actually part of your revision. It doesn't provide any new course content, just revising and reviewing. There's a lot to be said for taking at least a quick skim through it as soon as you can, just to get the measure of it.

(d) Most people tend to allocate the bulk of their time to block revision. But this activity reminds you to leave time for other modes of revision, all of which can be extremely helpful.

(e) There's no reason why you shouldn't use an ordinary calendar or diary if that's the way you like to work. But the electronic version does have the advantage of being easy to modify as your plans change.

(f) As indicated in *The Good Study Guide*, it's likely that you will have to change your revision plan as it is overtaken by events. But having something written down will help you to readjust strategically, rather than simply muddling along.

> My worry is time constraints. I have a full-time job with heavier than usual case load. Arrggh! I have decided that when the office is empty at week-ends I get so much more of my work done and as the house is manic at weekends I wouldn't study, so I will be working weekends to lessen my case load at work, then taking 2 days off in the week when the kids are at school and the house is quiet enough to study. I will be printing off a calendar and planning blocks of time, the majority of which is in the 2 days off, then shorter amounts of time for the rest of the 3 days – taking a complete break Saturday and Sunday evenings for family time. As for the blocks which I will be studying I will skim back through from the beginning and pick whatever I remember being interested in as I have most likely absorbed the majority of it already. If anyone understands what I've just explained I will be amazed!!! (But I feel better for saying it.)
>
> (Past student)

(g) Work with other students as much as you can. It's a very valuable way of keeping things in proportion.

Here are some comments about online collaboration from past students:

> 'The support was brilliant … the suggestions, advice and support from tutors and other students were great.'

> 'Without the online forums, I just didn't know how to start my revision. I could read the messages and if I didn't know what they were on about, I went back to the book.'

> 'Because the revision group was "chatty" you could ask anything without fear, which meant we asked a lot!'

> 'I thought everything about the online study support was excellent, it really helped me feel at ease beforehand. Pity you weren't all there in the exam with me though!'

If you stay in control of your revision activities, the revision period can be very rewarding. As you go back and revive ideas which were in your mind months ago, and see the connections with what you've done since, you will begin to feel a growing confidence in your new knowledge and a deepening of your understanding. It will help if you keep in mind the following two principles:

1 **Make revision meaningful and interesting**. Avoid letting it become boring. Seek out ways to make it active, enquiring, creative and varied.

2 **Play to your strengths**. Build on your interests and experience. Work to patterns that suit you. Don't worry about what you are not – be yourself. You are doing this for *you*.

When I have chosen the blocks to concentrate on, by skimming back thro' from the start, I think I will begin to look at the notes I made during my TMA prep. – I kept a file and noted the theorists, then their rationale of the subject, so I have a list of who said what and why. Then when I read back over a block I can think about the subject in hand, e.g. institutionalisation, and automatically remember that Goffman was the main man, and that he had the theory of total institutions and the inmate role, binary management etc.

(Past student)

Learning skills: Making yourself look ahead

I hope the activities and discussion have helped to put the K101 exam into perspective, making it seem more 'real' and, in a sense, 'ordinary' – something that will just happen one day, you will get on with it, then it will be over and part of your past – not a vague and mysterious threat looming over you. It's tempting to avoid thinking about the exam, but looking ahead is important. It's the way you develop the insight and learn the techniques that bring the best out of you.

3.2 Developing your writing skills

Now, as you approach your final assignment, it's time to review what you have achieved through the many hours you have spent thinking about and writing your essays in this course.

Learning to write the academic way

As you read in the Conclusion to Unit 19, higher knowledge takes the form of 'discourse'. Being knowledgeable is being able to join in an expert discourse and say things that make sense to other speakers of the discourse. That is why writing essays is such an important part of academic study. As you have written your K101 essays you have been practising using the academic discourse on health and social care to say things for yourself.

But you also read at the end of Unit 18 that academic writing is a special kind of discourse. It follows rules in order to search after truth. These are rules about logical argument and debate – about criticism and analysis – about evidence, objectivity and precision. So a key purpose of your essay writing has been to get practice in following these rules as best you could. Equally, a key part of your tutor's role has been to follow your arguments and give guidance on where they work well and where they could be strengthened.

Taking ideas you have read about in K101 and trying to use them to 'speak' thoughts of your own in the form of written sentences which lead logically from one to the next, following the academic rules, is the deepest learning you have done during the course. It will have been a struggle – that is the nature of learning – but you will have made a lot of progress. And having invested all that time and effort, it is worth going back over it all to review what you have gained.

DVD

Activity 12   How has your writing progressed during K101?

Allow about 30 minutes

To explore this question, find Block 5, Unit 20, Activity 12 on the DVD.

Comment

You should have found this a very useful exercise in setting yourself up for writing your final essay. But before you do that, there is one more aspect of writing that is worth thinking about – the intensity of the experience.

The experience of writing

Do you look forward to writing? Do you dread it? Or do you simply resign yourself to it? Is it perhaps a love/hate relationship – hugely demanding, but also quite rewarding to look back on? It would be surprising if writing was something you treated lightly. Many people feel it is like being put through an emotional wringer. Why should that be? As a student with perhaps several more years of writing ahead of you, can you cope with such intense experiences?

DVD   Reader

Activity 13   How do you react to the experience of writing?

Allow about 40 minutes

(a) To begin your exploration of this question, find Block 5, Unit 20, Activity 13 on the DVD and do the quiz there. This part of Activity 13 should take about 10 minutes.

(b) When you have completed the DVD activity you should have a printed copy of your answers about the feelings that essay writing arouses in you. The quiz questions relate to the topics in Section 11.5 of Chapter 11 of *The Good Study Guide*, pages 329 to 334.

Read Section 11.5 and see what light it casts on your quiz answers. You might want to revise some of your answers.

Comment

Having completed this activity you might like to visit the online forums and compare your thoughts about the emotional side of writing with those of other students. Writing is a lonely business, as even highly successful writers confirm – so it's helpful to know that other people experience the same anxieties and self-doubt when they write.

Reader

The very final task is to pull together all your writing development during the course, in preparation for your last essay, by reading the summary of Chapters 10 and 11 in *The Good Study Guide*. Read 'Taking control of writing', Section 11.6 of Chapter 11 of *The Good Study Guide*, pages 334 to 335.

End-of-block assignment

All that remains is for you to write the final assignment, TMA 07. You will find details in the Assessment Guide.

References

Website

www.statistics.gov.uk (Accessed 1 July 2008).

Course team

Production team

Andrew Northedge (Chair)

Joanna Bornat (Deputy Chair)

Corinne De Souza (Course Manager)

Maureen Richards (Course Manager)

Sarah Shelley (Course Team Assistant)

Dorothy Atkinson

Fiona Barnes

Ken Blakemore

Hilary Brown

Joyce Cavaye

Anne Fletcher

Marion Hall

Julia Johnson

Rebecca Jones

Ann Martin

Mo McPhail

Ingrid Nix

Sheila Peace

Mary Twomey

Jan Walmsley

Naomi Watson

Fran Wiles

Media production team

Phil Greaney, Fiona Harris, Matthew Moran, Jenny Nockles (Editorial Media Developers); Paul Bishop, Ray Guo (Interactive Media Developers); Vicky Eves (Graphic Artist); Debbie Crouch (Designer); Judy Thomas (Librarian); Adrian Bickers, Michelle Woolley (Media Project Managers); Philippa Broadbent, Ann Carter, Kim Dulson, Siggy Martin (Print Buyers); Sas Amoah, Bisiola Arogundade (Media Assistants); Martin Chiverton (Executive Sound and Vision Producer); Carole Brown (Sound and Vision Assistant); Gail Block, Melisa Ekdoghan, Phil Gauron, Annie Morgan (Clear Focus Productions); Lindsay Brigham, Phil Coleman (Integrated Vocational Route); Richard Norris, Harry Venning (Cartoonists).

External assessor

Jon Glasby, University of Birmingham

Critical readers

John Adams, James Blewett, Ian Buchanan, Barry Cooper, Celia Davies, Monica Dowling, Sarah Earle, Ric Estee-Wale, Elizabeth Forbat, Sandy Fraser, Sally French, Teresa Geraghty, Leonie Kellaher, Aine MacNamara, Mick McCormick, Paul McDonald, Ann Mitchell, Alun Morgan, Sam Parboteah, Vijay Patel, Jenny Pearce, Lucy Rai, Martin Robb, Angela Russell, Janet Seden, Patricia Taylor, Linda Walker, Anthea Wilson.

Developmental testers

John Dow, Tamsin Dunsdon, Trisha Shaw, Susan Underwood, Mark Vine.

Acknowledgements

Grateful acknowledgement is made to the following sources for permission to reproduce material in this book.

Text

Page 63: © Revill, J. (2005) 'Paperwork mountain keeps nurses from care', *Observer*, 27 September, p. 33.

Tables/illustrations/cartoons/other

Page 16 and 18: © GmbH & Co. KG/Alamy; page 22: © Sally & Richard Greenhill/Alamy; page 26: © Jim Varney/Science Photo Library; page 30 © Photofusion Picture Library/Alamy; page 35 © Mike Abrahams/Alamy; page 38: www.johnbirdsall.co.uk; page 46: © Ross Parry; page 75: © Powell, T; page 76: © Paul Schatzberger; page 80: © DOH; page 115: © Syner-Comm/ Alamy Images; page 120: © Janine Wiedel/Alamy Images; page 129: © Office for National Statistics.